BRONSON A

BY LEE WORTLEY AND PAULA WILLIAMSON

Mojo Risin'
Publishing Ltd

Published in 2021 by Mojo Risin' Publishing Ltd
www.mojorisinpublishing.com

British Library Cataloguing in Publication Data:
A catalogue record for this book is available from
the British Library

ISBN-13:
978-1-9163867-7-8

Cover design
David Stanyer

Layout & Copy Edit
Neil Jackson, Media Arts
www.media-arts.co.uk

Printed & bound by PrintGuy
Proudly published Up North

"I WANT OUR FACKIN' WEDDING PHOTO'S PAULA... OR SOME B'STARDS
GONNA GET HURT!"

"IF YOU'VE GOT ANYTHING TO SAY, YOU CAN TELL ME WHEN I GET OUT,
WHICH WILL BE SOONER THAN A LOT OF YOU THINK!"

"YEH, LET LENNY MCLEAN'S BOYS GO TA' WORK... THEN SEE IF THE
BULLIES WANNA' COME OUT TO PLAY!"

On behalf of myself and the whole Wortley family, I would just like to dedicate my work here to our late Aunty Tina.

Bless you sweetheart, to us you were 'Simply The Best.' x

Lee Wortley, March 2021.

Contents

Foreword By Charles Salvador	2
Writer's Notes One	3
Writer's Notes Two	4
Writer's Notes Three	7
Foreword By Hazel Williamson	12
Introduction	13
Dear Charlie	16
A Romantic New Age	22
The Blossoming Teen	25
Lapdancing My Way Through Drama School	30
A Star Is Born	38
Introduction To The Twins	41
Handlebar Moustache And A Dream	44
Charlie's Right Hand Woman	50
Pap And What The Rats See	58
The Gangster's Moll	61
Salvador's Personal Assistant	63
Salvador's Darlin'	69
I Do Thee Wed	85
Ticket For One Please	92
The Accidental Whipping Boy	99
They Tried To Make Me Go To Rehab	108
A Lorry Load Of Dreams	118
A Public Flogging	120
Too Late For Goodbyes'	125
Dedication By Peter Jones	130
Paula's Joy By Hazel Williamson	134

Foreword By Charles Salvador (in his own words and unedited)

Before Paula married me she was a very established woman with her own house, car, and was respected by many. She had beauty and brains. The media crap she got was totally out of order, but that's how it is being Mrs Bronson. It goes with the title.

Our wedding press was like royalty. It was so priceless nobody has seen the twenty-two photos I paid for. We are not even allowed them and they remain locked in a safe at Prison HQ. In my four and half decades of prison life I have only ever known of one other prisoner who was denied his wedding photos and that was Reggie Kray.

That's how it is when you're infamous. The system tries everything to mess you up and cause untold misery. Paula has a strong heart, but it even made her go mad and pushed her onto the edge of insanity. She came close to death, it cost her so much. It was cruel and barbaric and no wife deserves the crap she got. It's why you're reading this book, it's her turn now to put the truth out for the public to see the other side. A side that is at times suppressed and buried. Well now it's out once and for all for all to see the true facts.

Paula is a very flirtatious, sexy, naughty red-blooded woman. The only woman I can compare her to is Kelly Brook. Very similar in beauty, but Paula's sexier and naughtier and I am proud of our chapter in life together. Sure, we had our ups and downs, who don't? But our relationship was between three of us; me, her, and the prison security guard.

Unfortunately, prison controls us. Our calls are monitored, our mail censored, our visits take place with the highest of security. It's almost impossible to be a married couple and there is just no privacy. There is nothing but eyes, cameras, concrete and steel but we had a magical ride. We had fun and games and no regrets. Paula will always be a part of my journey of life.

I just want to make it one hundred per cent clear now before the rats run out of the sewers that this book you are about to read was actually my idea, not Paula's. My reason for that is to put her side over and how she had a great journey of life before we ever met, and I believe her best years are yet to come.

When you get to the end of the book, I think you'll agree she is a legend in her own lifetime. Did you know there's an Arab Prince who keeps asking her to fly out to his palace? Did you know there's a multi-millionaire businessman who proposed to her no less than six times? Did you know she's been offered one million bucks to do a porno movie?

I could go on and on, but this is Paula's story. It's insane but all true and I hope you enjoy it. I predict she will end up everybody's favourite fun girl once the British public see through the darkness that's surrounded her through the Paula-Bronson myth. You will then see the true beauty. just give her a chance as she has earnt her respect the hard way.

Charlie Salvador 2019

Writer's Notes One

Unfortunately, a few months after Charlie submitted his foreword to us the unforeseen happened and Paula sadly passed away. In the weeks leading up to Paula's passing she appeared extremely morose and became overtly obsessed with her own mortality; so much so that she even said to me: "Lee, if I drop dead through the night please carry on where we have left off, and please get my story published."

Previous to this in the May of 2019, I had instructed Paula to write down her story in brief overview format so that I could, in due course, work on it and get it publisher ready. This she did to her best ability and the contents of her text gave me enough material to work from. These extensive, handwritten notes of some 20,000 words briefly covered the peaks and troughs of her entire life. And using this and voice recordings between myself, Peter Jones, Beverleigh Zacher and Star Darke I managed to tell the whole story.

So now, after the best part of a year of working tirelessly, it is ready for public viewing. However, on completion, there was one last thing I needed to do: I needed to contact Charlie Salvador (her husband) and ask if he still agreed to us using the foreword he wrote and sent to Paula before she passed. Today, the 26th July, 2020, I received a message from his prison cell saying:

"Hey Lee, I've done the forward ages ago, mate… go with it, no problem! I've got a lot of things on now: I got me' jam-roll (parole) coming up, it's looking good! I could be out next year. Ya' know I loved her - respected her, she was a good girl, sad ending… not nice, I still miss her, as does my George. I loved her, mate. Good luck… 'ope it's a winner.
Charlie!"

Writer's Notes Two

The following is an audio transcript between me, the protagonist Paula Salvador and her husband, Charlie Salvador. This was recorded at the height of their union and gives you an insight, straight from the man, into how he felt about the new love in his life, Paula:

Paula: Hello Lee, I absolutely loved the chatterview interview (Gangland Podcast) and I've got someone here who wants to say … thanks for doing a good job.

Charlie: Hey Lee, nice one mate … yeh, 'ope it turns out well! Ain't I got a diamond eh? Now see why I'm behavin' me self. Since she's come into me' life: I got nuffin' but 'ope; bit o' love in me 'eart. Feel good! Got every 'ing to be 'ave for.

Paula: Yes, you have!

Charlie: Get out there, 'ave some fun … love 'er to pieces, respect her! She's an absolute angel.

Paula: Aww, thank you.

Charlie: Ave fell on me feet mate! Yeh, nice one Lee, nice one mate; it's nice to 'ave people like you in our corner, mate
.
Paula: Yeh, definitely, definitely!

Charlie: We'll 'ave to invite him to the party ya' know Paula?

Paula: We will … you and Ant: Ant's the other one. Erm … Haha the other one! Erm … yes, they'll both be invited.

Charlie: Did you tell Lee where we're 'avin the 'oneymoon?

Paula: I'm sure I … yeh! But you tell him as well.

Charlie: 'Ere Lee, get on this mate, you'll fackin' lav (love) this! My mate Andy Jones, he owns and runs Littledean Jail Museum; down in Littledean, Gloucestershire. It's a prison: a fourteen, fifteenth century prison, an' Andy's got me a cell darn there: beautiful cell! Be like 'ome from 'ome. Anyway, see that cell? That's our 'oneymoon suite mate! Andy's gonna lock us in for a couple o' nights.

Paula: How about that?

Charlie: Haha … is that fackin' wicked, or is that wicked? It's absolute, brilliant!

Paula: Only you…

Charlie: Ya' couldn't make it up! But what ya' gotta realise, Lee. See a cell to me … a cell. (Charlie whispered) Don't get me wrong now … I'm not institution-alised! I fackin' 'ate (hate) prison! I'm never gonna be institutionalised! You don't rip off nine prison roofs' and take eleven hostages' and become institutionalised!

Charlie: But! 'Avin said that, see that little cell down in Littledean Jail? When I get bored, or fed up … It'll do me the world o' good just ta' pop down there for a couple o' days, or a couple o' weeks.'

Paula: I'll put you in there!

Charlie: Andy can lock me up! That's our 'oneymoon suite mate. I'm like a lion mate, in the jungle; that's my domain.

Charlie: And ya' know what? See Paula, she will lav (love) it in there.

Paula: I will!

Charlie: She will lav (love) it; ya' not gonna get an 'otel in the world better than that! Max secure! (He fiendishly giggled)

Charlie: Anyway, you're one of a few to know that; we ain't told too many, but that's our 'oneymoon suite, mate. Alright mate, all the best, 'ope it goes well.

Paula: Speak to you soon, Lee. Hope you enjoyed that!
With that, the Prison gate slammed, and Charlie was gone.

Charlie: Andy can lock me up! That's our 'oneymoon suite mate. I'm like a lion mate, in the jungle; that's my domain.

Charlie: And ya' know what? See Paula, she will lav (love) it in there.

Paula: I will!

Charlie: She will lav (love) it; ya' not gonna get an 'otel in the world better than that! Max secure! (He fiendishly giggled)

5

Charlie: Anyway, you're one of a few to know that; we ain't told too many, but that's our 'oneymoon suite, mate. Alright mate, all the best, 'ope it goes well.

Paula: Speak to you soon, Lee. Hope you enjoyed that!

With that, the Prison gate slammed, and Charlie was gone.

Writer's Notes Three

A little while before Paula and Charlie's engagement, Paula recorded her fiancée revealing his hopes and dreams and what he had planned for the two of them after his release.
The following is the word-for-word transcript:

Paula: Yeh!

Charlie: Go on?

Paula: Go on then? Erm, I just want to know, people are interested obviously, so I just want to know, about me and you; about our future and how you see things?

At which point Charlie interrupted while going into song, singing, 'So happy together' by the Turtle's and Fern Kinney's 'We are Beautiful' changing the lyrics from he into she appropriately, while Paula chuckled along all modest and agreeable in the background…

Charlie: Go on then? Right, my Paula … me and Paula. What can ya' say? I'll tell you what I can say, she's bladdy lavvly! She's gorgeous … she's delicious. She smells good … she tastes good … she is good.
Our future, it's beautiful and there's thing's I could say, but I'm not gonna say, because … it's a secret.

Paula: It is!

Charlie: We got good news … no bad news.

Paula: All good news!

Charlie: Fantastic news …we've even got, yeh, yeh, exclusive this! We've even gone and booked up our honeymoon.

Paula: Oh Lord.

Charlie: Yeh …Littledean Prison! He proclaimed as the pair of them chuckled. I've even got my own cell, oh by the way, Littledean Prison is about four hundred years old and my mate owns it – he's turned it into a museum. He's kept me a cell 'asn't he … I've got me' own flowery dell d'arn there. And that's where we're 'avin our 'oneymoon!

Paula: Lucky me! (Laughing)

Charlie: Andy Jones who owns it is a lavvly man and a good friend o' mine. He's gonna' lock us up for our 'oneymoon. It's gonna' be gorgeous ...for me it's gonna' be 'ome-from- 'ome init'!

Paula: It is!

Charlie: Yeh, we've got lavvly plans – erh, dreams! Erh, put it like this: When I get out ...and it's gonna' be sooner that a lot of people think. Yeh, there's gonna' be some arses twitching, mate, w'en they see I'm gettin' out. Believe me ...there's a lot of people out there who have used and abused me ya' know - yeh ... used my name.

Paula: Mmmm

Charlie: Yeh, that's why I killed off Bronson and become Charlie Salvador. 'Cos I'm a born-again artist...

Charlie: Anyway, my Paula ... what are we gonna' do outside?

Paula and Charlie: What aren't we gonna' do!

Charlie: That's the question. Erh, we're gonna' do fings' (things), nice fings'! Put on some art shows and do plenty o' charity.

Paula: We want to do a lot of work: a lot of good, and we obviously want our private time as well ... erm.

Charlie: Little co'age (cottage) by the sea and we can call it Rainbow Co'age!

Paula: Rainbow Cottage. She reiterates humorously. That's why we want two cottages. Erm ... a place in London for a bit of business and, somewhere else which no one will know about.

Charlie: And the reason we want a little co'age out in the coun'ry (country), is because that's where I wanna' create my masterpiece art.

Paula: Yes, in the garden.

Charlie: I was recently asked by a very prominent journalist, who will remain, nameless; 'cos he's done me a lot of favours over the years – he's a gentleman! Anyway, he said to me: 'Charles' (in a whispered, subdued voice) ... that's how talks by the way. 'Charles,' he said, 'what is the greatest art you've created up until now?'

And I fought (thought) about it … and I fought to myself … It's not been created yet mate!

Paula: Exactly!

Charlie: And it won't be created until I'm sitting in my garden, in our little Rainbow Co'age, creating the masterpiece! He announces, vigorously.

Paula: And it will be.

Charlie: It's gonna' be a masterpiece 'cos it's gonna' be done in a very special way. And I'll leave the rest for my Paula to describe how?

Paula: I don't know if I can, on this. (Laughing)

Charlie: She might not describe how because it's very, very, 'eavy!

Paula: And naughty … but we can't give everything away…

Charlie: Nice, naughty – nice, naughty!

Paula: Naughty but nice. But listen, one of the thing's I'd like us to talk about, is, a lot of people in this country think we're a publicity stunt…

Charlie: Right, do ya' want me to answer that? It's a load o' bollocks! An absolute load o' bollocks. Er, what we are … we were two lost souls, like two leaves' floating in a tornado, and we've just landed together. And since we've been together everything's been lavvly.

Paula: It has … it's clicked into place.

Charlie: I feel 'appy, contented, I feel good … all my madness and badness and violence has disappeared, I just feel relaxed, chilled out, mature, I'm acting me age. 'Cos I have been naughty ya' know? Very naughty…

Paula: You have … you've been a little bit naughty, yes.

Charlie: You don't do forty-free (three) years in the can (Jail) for being good, do ya'?
But I now feel I've come to that time in me' life when I need a bit o' spoonin'!

Paula: And you're going to have it.

Charlie: I need a bit o' lav (love) in me' life?

Paula: Yes, and you're definitely going to have it.

Charlie: I need a bit o' naughtiness, too.

Paula: You've got it … don't you worry about that.

Charlie: At the end of the day, the people that write shit, and talk shit, well they become shit, don't they?

Paula: It's jealousy. They don't have a lot going on in their own lives and have to throw the, whatever, at someone else, don't they?

Charlie: It's like these Facebook warriors. Ooh … they make my skin crawl; they really do when they sit behind their computers. Incidentally, I've never even seen a computer let alone work one. But they sit behind their screens wi' (with) their little fingers goin' … dribbling at the mouth – who can I upset, today? And then they're all like little sheep jumpin' on the bandwagon; like a load of rats steaming down the sewer … yeh, brave ain't they? Ain't they brave? They all gang up on one person … like my Paula, like they 'ave done in the past.

Paula: Well, they've tried to.

Charlie: They've tried … but they got a little bit more than the bit orf (off), didn't they? Now they're not naughty, no! I call them, evil!

Paula: I just call them pathetic; I just think I feel sorry for 'em.

Charlie: They're bullies!

Paula: It's just bullying tactics!

Charlie: That is bullying, and I hate 'em!

Paula: I mean, Charlie's had shit thrown at him in the past; probably literally and figuratively, erm, and now, I'm getting shit thrown at me. And it's ridiculous; I don't deserve it: we are the real deal. If a bird meets a footballer and she goes out with him, does she get the shit thrown at her, no she doesn't.

Charlie: Good question that, Paula!

Paula: Just because I've fallen in love with someone, who happens to be notorious and in prison, that does not make me a bad person … or anything else.

Charlie: First time me and Paula met – actually it was an open visit wasn't it?

Paula: It was an open visit, yeh.

Charlie: And I've been on closed visits for decades.

Paula: So that was strange.

Charlie: That first visit … when our eyes met each other. We melted into each other. It was absolutely gorgeous.

Paula: And I didn't know if you felt the same way. But you know what? Anyone who doubts me and you I'd like to give them five minutes watching the two of us together, because they'd walk out and go, pfft, these two are meant to be.

Charlie: It's the real deal … it's the real deal there's no doubt about it. Me' life has changed, there's a rainbow above me 'ead now. There was always blackness, and greyness and darkness, 'orribleness. But now, I wake up in the morning, smiling. I do me workouts; I do me art … I feel good, I bounce about, feel alive, fit, well, 'appy, I've got a future … c'mon! And I'm living in an 'annibal Lecter cage. I've been locked in an 'annibal Lecter cage for most o' me' life, and all of a sudden, I'm 'appy.

At which point, once again Charlie bursts into song, reciting the lyrics of Ken Dodd and Happiness!

Charlie: 'Two little boys, had two little toys, each 'ad a wooden hor…' Ooh, I'd better not sing that song, 'cos its bloody Rolf 'arris init, bloody Rolf 'arris. Ere do ya' remember back in the 60s, him singing that song: Two little Boys' … yeh, well we all know now what he was singing about don't we? Now he is nasty!

Foreword By Hazel Williamson (Mum)

Paula had been making notes on her life since studying at Manchester University on the Performing Arts degree course around the turn of the millennium. Initially it was no more than a private hobby but later it metamorphosized into an obsessive desire for her to explain her life.

After falling in love with and marrying Britain's number one criminal behind bars, Charles Salvador, she was subjected to severe bullying by the underclasses who not only berated, scorned and harassed her relentlessly but who also continually issued death threats', anonymously, of course, being cowards.

Paula was a star who shone with unbelievable brilliance and beauty but not far below the surface of the effervescent glamour there was a very frail and frightened soul plagued with a serious psychological disorder.

This female, Paula, had the middle Christian name of Joy and this is what she brought to all of us who knew her well. I speak for myself and many others: we just didn't realise how very vulnerable our girl was and that for her, life could not be sustained for the natural span.

Introduction

My life has never been on an even keel. I've always trodden a different path along life's wobbly roads which, to the average soulless creature, could be deemed questionable. But listen, I'm only here once, and wanted to make a mark in a way I saw fit, and it would appear that from an early age my mind and ideals where completely set in stone.

I remember my mum telling me that while we were holidaying one year (I must have been about 6 or 7 years old) a lady in her twilight years asked: "So my dear, what do you want to be when you grow up?" To which I rather boldly replied: "RESPECTED!" I bet she thought, clever little sod, as she smiled through gritted teeth and went on her merry way. But this is me, it is simply the way I was made. And make no mistake, looking back at the girl with the cheeky smile and pigtails it was quite obvious from that day forward that I would one day get noticed. However, the path fate had chosen for me was yet to be written.

Never before has there been a more candid and concise story written about Britain's most fabled and infamous prisoner, Charles Bronson! The fact that in the year 2014 he changed his surname to Salvador, with the flaky hope of escaping his handwoven, notorious and violent namesake, meant nothing whatsoever to the haters and powers that be. Bronson would forever remain entombed, mind, body, and soul, branded with the 'Bronson' moniker. A name that today, and for the rest of his days would summon up negative images; a name that serves as a tool for the hierarchy to use as a distinct-warning to any other rebellious up-comer with a similar criminal remit.

Once our union was bonded by marriage, I, Paula Williamson took on his 2014 deed-pole legal surname of 'Salvador' in the hope of helping distance the man from the myth. However, to the media and tabloids, this thinly veiled name change had no effect whatsoever, for 'Bronson,' as a brand, was a far more lucrative commodity, a media-driven cash cow that I would soon, reluctantly, be a part of.

Charlie himself remains locked away in a high security prison, with a glut of sycophantic gofers on the other side of the wall waiting with breath-bated to carry out his every instruction. For a time, I served as his right-hand woman (no pun intended) and in that time I witnessed a man that got exactly what he wanted, unless of course, you are me, a woman who at times dared to utter the word "No!" to this fearsome and animated figure.

Yes, that's right, me, Paula Salvador (Williamson), the girl right here dictating my thoughts to my writer and friend, Lee. A woman that once trod water in the tentative realms of Charlie's inner sanctum. A woman who single-handedly created a delirium of media attention that spread far-and-wide across our green and pleasant land as I said, "I do," at the prison's alter in November of 2017.

Since our engagement on Valentine's Day of the same year, a

tsunami of excitement spread like wildfire to a sensationalising media, this group of people who had waited impatiently in the hope of being the first to get me in front of a camera to tell my story. Because, for the hungry world of journalism, questions needed answering: questions such as: 'Why on earth would an up-and-coming actress and drama tutor marry a monster like Bronson?'

Of course, most sceptics among the listeners and readers instantly thought I was in desperate need of a profile-raiser to aid my climb of prominence to its zenith. However, fortunately for me, the majority watched from a less judgemental vantage point which revealed a less injurious belief. But hey, who gives a bugger about the positive ones! Because, you see, the nicer version of events serves up no spice whatsoever.

In fact, the judging minority seemed too overwhelmingly blinded by the superficial lies to produce even a modicum of truth from the real evidence. And this for me was gruelling, as I tried to keep the accumulation of daily letters, calls, and visits that I had to endure as private as possible. Nonetheless, once word leaked out, I was unavoidably sacked from every job, immediately removed from my daily TV position on Judge Rinder and kicked to the proverbial curb by my agent.

Therefore, with time on my hands I adopted the role of Charlie's confidante, dealing with the press and media and organising protest marches at the Ministry of Justice, and 10 Downing Street. And, with my little army of Charlie supporters, I took to the London streets and armed with a loud hailer and a signature scrawled petition of 22,000 we fought the good fight, for Charlie's plight.

In addition to this, I dealt with the numerous charities and individuals that Charlie's namesake aids. Nevertheless, riding the 'crest-of-a-wave' alongside Charlie's yes men proved no easy task. And, during this unholy debacle, the great British public watched on; perplexed, bewildered, and concerned, as one of the country's most kooky weddings unfolded before them, and soon after, scoffed and mocked its expeditious demise.

Then came the breakdown on live TV, at a time when I was last seen heading for rehab after suffering an alcohol and prescription drug problem. But what really happened during rehabilitation? Not to mention, the reasons for its abrupt end that I will disclose in the final print. Furthermore, why did Charlie put a request in for me to visit him, while ignoring pleas with the promise of hard cash from a mass of admirers who simply wanted to meet their idol?

What is the truth behind those visits, visits conducted in front of a discretely coaxed guard? Why the intrigue into this busty brunette with the big green eyes, and why was I equally intrigued as well? Also, what made a girl who had been saving herself for that 'special man' pick a man like Bronson?

Furthermore, what truly happened on their wedding day? In addition to all the above, who was the illusive 'pap boy', who followed my every move, George Bamby, who sometime after sat in front of Eamonn and Ruth on national TV claiming to have sprung from Charlie's loins.

So, as the dirty cash grew for the 'pap', so did the meat on my bones, adding weight, if you will, to a relentless and overpowering onslaught of cyber-bullying. And with threats of violence and a gun to my head meant my anxiety swiftly escalated. Which in turn compelled me to sift through my little black book of "naughty contacts" and call upon a friend and colleague of the late Guv'nor Lenny McLean. And as a result, was immediately thrust under the protection of a fearsome and formidable right-hand-man, known simply to me at that time as 'The Neck!'

So, what really went on behind the scenes of Britain's answer to the odd couple, and what was really behind that tabloid argument that followed the announcement of their separation; an action that 'just 72 hours later' led to Charlie romancing his next lady friend. The ex-girlfriend of Simon Cowell named Jasmine Lennard, who boosted an overwhelming degree of cyberbullying when I was at my lowest ebb.

So, are we really divorced, and what is stopping me going after the cash he has pugged away? Is he ever getting out? And why do I still draw in so many followers of my own? Was it a stunt pulled off to perfection or was it the true story of a damaged, albeit tough northern girl who was simply the subject of exploitation? One thing is certain, in this poignant and revealing expose this girl pulls no punches, as I impart this story, with no unturned stone, as I, for the very first time reveal in my own unique and flavoursome way, gold dust, that for a few years I held back from a salivating nation.

Why now I hear you say? Why a reveal all, expose book? Well, for a start, it was Charlie that initially came up with the idea, and furthermore hon-oured it by writing one of the book's forewords.

There you have it, a literary box-ticking feast; a thesis, served up for your scrutiny and judgment. The story of Charlie and Paula Salvador's union, from beginning to end with nothing left unsaid. What was it like being married to the country's most dangerous prisoner? And what really happened during their two-hour prison wedding? Prepare yourself to be shocked, for this thing is just about to get tasty!

Chapter One: Dear Charlie...

Is it me? Am I delusional? Am I the only one on this wretched planet who feels this way? Am I losing the plot? Scratch that, rather, did I ever have it in my possession in the first bloody place?

It can't be just me. I'm a well-rounded girl! A pillar of the community! Ok, so that last proclamation was, to coin a cockney phrase, strongin' it a bit. But I've always been on the right side of the law; well let's just say that during my days spent on this mortal coil I've teetered delicately on the cusp of it. What I mean to say is, OK, so I've purchased the odd gross of dodgy 'Coco Chanel' from time to time, well a girls gotta smell nice hasn't she? And yes, I've smoked a bit of Bob's favourite foliage as I tripped and stumbled my way through my teens. Nevertheless, for the most part, as George Bernard Shaw's Ms Doolittle immovably squawked: "I'm a good girl I am!"

However, this is my life, and the only one I have. So, why then do I feel forever harassed and tortured by everyone else's opinions of me. When, as my mother undoubtedly informs me: "Listen my dear, the only opinion that actually counts for anything is mine, and your father's. Isn't that right Clive?" "Clive, please try and divert your eyes from that new blonde girl on Countdown for a second! I'm trying to have a serious conversation with our daughter here..." Having said that, if your own loving mother and father aren't championing you in your passion for life and its very survival, no bugger else will. Even though my parents haven't always been behind me on my journey into what has been an extreme and at times catastrophic lust-for-life, they were always there to catch me if ever I fell.

The year was 2015 and having not long finished my regular work in Manchester, I headed off to the Arndale shopping centre for a bit of light retail therapy. Mind you, I say 'therapy,' but for me trailing around shops carrying loads of bags, isn't exactly how I'd refer to it! Nonetheless, it was a calling; there must have been a snappy little number in the form of a dress I needed for an event or something.

Anyway, I remember walking past Topshop and throwing my bags down in a 'Nikki Graeme from Big Brother' style strop and saying out loud: "Enough! I'm bloody exhausted; I feel like a sodding pack horse with this lot!" When suddenly, there in front of me a beacon of hope beckoned: A pulp-filled sanctuary, Waterstones. You see, I've always been an avid reader, in particular true crime, autobiographies, biographies and such like. Therefore, once again, I eased myself back into the guise of Nikki Graeme and trundled my way towards the shop, complaining all the way that flats would've been a more appropriate choice of footwear as opposed to boots with a big bloody heel, 'cos my trotters (feet) had had quite enough!

As I walked into the bookshop, I gasped an overdramatic huff; which quickly drew the attention of a staff member who asked if I required any assistance? "Yes!" I demanded, "A cold bloody chardonnay, a foot massage, and a fluffy pillow to rest my weary head would be ideal!" Well, that's what I thought of saying. But instead, respond with no, and that I was perfectly fine and knew exactly what I was looking for.

About halfway down on the right-hand side was the true crime section. I immediately threw my bags to the floor and began studying and scrutinising the shelves 'Got that, and that, and that...' I said to myself rather disheartened; until my eyes made their way to the bottom shelf and one book stood out with the bold title, 'Broadmoor: My Journey into Hell'. The title alone immediately got my interest but then I saw the authors face, with his bald head and infamous handlebar-moustache staring back at me... 'God not him!' I thought to myself, as a shiver took over my body. 'That's that Charlie Bronson lunatic!' I had no interest in him whatsoever, he's that violent thug, I have zero psychological interest in him (how wrong I was!)

Anyway, I instantly dismissed it and began inspecting the shelves again. When suddenly, nope, this man would have to do! You see, at this point, I was desperate to sit down! So, I picked up the hardback book with his 'boat race' (face) and fists-up splashed across the front, shook my head negatively yet quickly, deciding that he may provide me with some comfort from the madness of a busy shopping centre, because as it would appear from the back cover synopsis, this boy had a tale or two to tell.

Only six months prior to this day I had suffered a mental breakdown and as a result was admitted to a psychiatric hospital, but more of that later. Anyway, despite its author, the title and narrative given in the synopsis intrigued me enough to pull out my flexible friend and shove it in the assistant's slot. *My my, what a filthy mind you have! Now, calm yourselves down a bit, I'll get to the juicy stuff later!*

At this point I ordered myself a cup of tea (strong with two sugars) and sat in the comfiest chair I could find. Ahhh thank God for this, I mused, as I took a swig of the comforting tea while opening the book. I flicked through it at first and despite being drawn to the artwork that I found fascinating, I was drawn to a beautiful picture of Charlie and Lorraine Etherington with the under title, 'Gotcha – with my Soulmate and Saviour, Lorraine.' They looked incredibly happy, moreover, he looked nothing like the man in the menacing cover photo. With that, I quickly read the back page about the two of them and was surprised to see that Charlie was now "anti-violent" and had raised thousands of pounds for charity. Had I judged this man a little too quickly and harshly? Perhaps I had, anyway, I felt instantly happy that he was now free with his fiancé Lorraine; they looked like a lovely pair.

Intrigued to know a little more about her I quickly read Lorraine's forward and discovered that he wasn't free at all; the man was still incarcerated - I was confused and needed to know more. So, I turned the page and started to read Charlie's words, he has a unique writing style that states facts while affording the reader a rare glimpse into his soul; what is more he doesn't mess about. I like people who say it (or in this case write it) as it is.

Both Loraine's foreword and Charlie's introduction had sent a chill down my spine. I felt as though I was holding something bloody special. I took another gulp of tea. Then had a casual flick through the book while scanning certain parts, and immediately my attention was held in a chokehold by his humour; a similar humour to mine, that leapt from the pages like a pop-up book. Momentarily, any thought of fatigue that I first felt was washed away, and that was it, I needed to get home and read this thing properly!

I rushed to the exit, leaving a half-drunk cup of tea on the table. Now, anyone that knows me would tell you that I never leave anything: I'm a Northerner and we don't leave anything behind, especially a cup of tea (ever!) so let us just say that that book must have resonated, hard.

I arrived home and dropped my bags by the front door and once my heavy bloody boots were off my feet, I could finally give the book the attention it evidently deserved. I settled on the sofa, curled up and began trawling through it like a dose of salts. As usual, I remember my phone going off with texts from my mates telling me of their antics through the day - yet for once my reply was delayed as I was engrossed in the text. I just couldn't stop reading it, and the people sending messages probably thought I was a right ignorant sod, as I read page after page with no reply to the messages before finally staggering off to bed. And even then, the book came with me; I propped up two pillows in front of me, making a trench for to rest its spine as read on until my eyes finally lost the battle over my eagerness to continue.

Fortunately, the next day was my day off. Well, I say day-off, but every day is usually filled to bursting with my itinerary. I've always been the same, although I'm not a morning person, I can be a moody shit until I've had my cuppa and entered the land of the living, however, the very next day my mood seemed a little different. I woke up bright-eyed, fed the cats, prepared my cup of rosy lee (tea) and headed back up to bed for round two. I picked up the book and started to read it again, this time even more ferociously, laughing and crying as somehow, I completely identified with it.

Now, I know that sounds crazy, but let me try and explain. Well, I've used humour through my life, I laugh at myself every day and in the past, my sense of humour has got me through some extremely dark times. My favourite saying, 'What a farce' accents the way I look at life, and for that, my philosophy is: if you can't laugh at yourself, then you need to remove the deep-sunken stick from up your aris (arse).

Now, I've not been in a straitjacket, or forcibly injected with a 'liquid cosh' or met the 'loons' that were depicted in the film 'Bronson', that was printed to film in 2008. However, I have lived a very colourful life and one dark time was being detained in hospital for my own safety not too long back. I have met some rather interesting people. In fact, in life the eccentric folk have always seemed to flock to my side like bees to a hive; to be honest, I think they can sense that I'm not quite 'normal' myself, I've a good heart and I care deeply for others, but I've always felt like an outsider. I've never really fitted in. And, as I've walked through life, I've never felt the bloody desire to. The fact of the matter is this, I like being me, and for me, Charlie came across in the exact same way.

So, the day came when I finally finished the book, and in case you were thinking what a filthy cow, I did make it out of bed to shower etc, and by the time nightfall was upon me I had devoured the whole bloody thing from cover to cover. And to my surprise was left feeling totally uplifted. The way it made me feel was that if this man could go through all that he has, and still come out smiling, then I can certainly handle the depressive demons that swirl around my mind on a daily and nightly basis.

Now, up to this point, I was simply another reader of his book, and the idea of ever contacting the protagonist could not be further from my mind. Nevertheless, I must admit that I fell to sleep that night feeling extremely grateful to him for authoring the book, and the devastating insomnia I'd suffered for such a long time seemed to have vanished. And for now, at least, my desperate need for pills and or alcohol as an aid to relax had become a distant memory: for Charlie had unintentionally cured me.

It was an early start for me the next day having to make my daily commute to Manchester. All through the day, I couldn't get his words out of my head. I just couldn't understand why he was still incarcerated, and once I arrived home later that day, good old Google provided me with the relevant information. Now, I'm not condoning certain things that Charlie has done in the past, but here, we seemed to have a man, who was for all intents and purposes anti-violent. Charlie seemed content, with a loving fiancé, and a passion and desire to produce original artwork – not to mention his tireless work for the many charities he supported and his deity, which of course was his fitness.

Suddenly, a little thought came creeping into my head, write to him Paula and thank him for writing such a fantastic book! Nevertheless, I immediately dismissed the idea as ridiculous. Although I pondered for a while thinking to myself, *'Look, he is an infamous character who probably receives letters by the hour, so why the hell would he be in the slightest bit interested in you?'*

It's worth noting that at this stage that I hadn't even seen the film 'Bronson' and if I had, perhaps I would have never written to him. However, I'm a girl who trusts her gut instincts and thought that the least I could do was send him a letter of thanks for writing 'Broadmoor.' So, that was that … my mind was made up, and that night I put pen to paper:

Dear Charlie,
First and foremost, 'is it okay to call you that?' Seems a bit familiar! Hope you don't mind. Right, where do I start… as I'm sure you get inundated with letters!

Well, my name is Paula and I recently read your book 'Broadmoor: My Journey Into Hell' and oh my god, it has hit me from all sides. I've pissed myself at some of your stories and cried at other parts, but most of all what I want to say is that it has really helped me. I've had a bit of shit not too long ago and had a mental breakdown and whilst I'm feeling a lot better than I did, your book has helped me no end! I thought that if you can go through all that and come out smiling, then so can I!

Congratulations on your engagement too, by the way, hopefully you can be out soon and be together, I'm glad you have someone special. I'll be honest, before reading your book I didn't know a lot about you, I think I must've thought you were a murderer because you've been inside for as long as I've been alive. I also thought you were just some violent thug, but I can see that there's a lot more to you. I judged you and I don't normally judge people, so for that I must apologise.

I'll follow your case and wish you all the best, seems like you've done your sodding time and then some! Anyway, I would truly like to thank you for writing the book, because it has really helped me mentally and was bloody funny too! Keep up the good work, your artwork is amazing and it's fabulous that it has raised so much for charity!

Bright Blessings,

Paula x

The very next day I popped it in the post box and thought that was that: I'd thanked him and felt content in my head that I had. And afterwards, life simply resumed as everything went back to normal, whatever the hell 'normal' means.

You see, in my life no two days are the same. By day, I worked as an actress, which meant attending castings, mainly for commercials, some that I got, some I didn't, that's just the way it goes in the land of TV, and even to dip your toe in the world of TV you needed a very thick skin, which is handy because mine is thicker that a rhino's. I'd had small parts in most of the mainstream soaps including, Coronation Street, Hollyoaks, Emmerdale, which was fantastic experience, and I had had a small role in the cop drama, Scott & Bailey, too.

In 2011 I was fortunate enough to play a journalist, Kirsty Stephens in the critically acclaimed 'Appropriate Adult' for ITV. This was a memoir about the evil killers Fred and Rose West. However, my main bread and butter was corporate videos (you know the ones when you have to have Health and Safety Training and you sit there trying not to fall asleep as you are made to watch it). Well, I got lots of work playing parts in those, 'The Lady Boss' part who you don't mess with (I must have one of those faces; bless you for that!)

I also worked in the role-playing arena, for various training companies to train their students and staff. Oh, and I did a bit of teaching too; it was varied, but as long as I was working, I was happy; I was very proactive, with the mantra 'if you want something in life you have to get off your arse and get it,' being something I adhered to. Opportunities just don't come knocking at your door, so you have to get in among the action - unless you win the postcode lottery of course! I'm also like a dog with a bone; I think it comes from a need to prove myself, for the simple fact that I never felt anyone ever believed in me; a stigma that runs through my bones so often it now seems part of my makeup.

Chapter Two: A Romantic New Age

So, let's go back to the beginning. I grew up in a modest, rural, two-up, two-down rented house in the roughest area of Stoke-on-Trent. I'm sort of half Manc and half Brum, so let's face it, my life was buggered from the get-go.

The announcement that I wanted to be an actress was met with immediate cynicism: I am of course being polite – 'cos they laughed their bloody heads off. I wanted dance lessons, but Mum and Dad simply couldn't afford it, so that kind of entertainment, instead, had to come from having a laugh with my mates, singing, dancing, and pretending to be Madonna. We also built extravagant dens and had a good scrap (fight) but were always home for my tea. (that's dinner to anyone south of Stoke) But then, as soon as tea was history I would be back out on the streets with my pals for more jollity!

I'm the youngest of seven children, and as such was given a loose set of rules to abide by but that was that. My parents just wanted me to be a child, not a child who was forever insistent on partaking in after-school clubs and all that kind of stuff. (To be honest, back in the 80s, I don't think that kind of thing hardly existed!) Well it didn't round my neck of the woods.

As a young child I was painfully shy. So shy in fact, I would hide up my mum's skirt if anyone even so much as spoke to me. One day over the Easter break, I said to my mum "Right, it's about time I reinvented myself!" To be honest, I don't even think I knew what the word meant! Incidentally, and thanks to Madonna, the Queen among Queens, I now have the phrase 'Reinvent Yourself' tattooed on the back of my neck. Anyway, around this time I quickly came out of my shell, which was extremely apt indeed, especially as it was Easter! So, that was that, my personality changed overnight. Now, for the simple fact that this is a memoir and not a biography, I shall refrain from going into heavier detail; let's just say that for now, I think a little toe-dip into my background history will act as a tool to help you understand people like myself and my husband Charlie.

During the early part of my youth, I realised that having fun and having the ability to make people laugh was something that came naturally to me, and this is why later in life I turned my attentions to comedy, which is something I'll touch on later. Growing up I moved schools quite a lot, which was all due to me being bullied and my mum leaving my Dad, then later moving back in with him simply because I missed him terribly; for my sake alone, Mum moved back in with Dad, yet was never truly happy and this remains a truth, even to this day, and it's something that I harbour a certain amount of guilt over. However, I was only 8 years old and because of this didn't realise how unhappy my mum actually was.

Mum is from a more well to do family to that of my dad and was the one who instilled the importance of education in me from such an early age. Mum is a fabulous character. She dresses immaculately and has a wonderful sense of dry northern wit. On the other side of the coin, is my dad: Dad is ex-army, and overbearingly old school. My Dad has an altogether different mantra in life to that of my mum, and when I was a young girl, I remember him telling me to always get the first punch in! A mantra that I equipped myself with from the first day he said it. Mind you, I hated the war films he used to play on repeat with tiresome consistency. One vivid recollection I have is of a man being flogged on a ship, Dad would rewind it on our VHS tape recorder (which took a million years) and play it again and again, unremittingly. I remember getting upset over the man on the TV getting hurt, having to hear his screams of pain got to me, and it was at this point that something was born in me that made me want to protect people - males and females alike, it didn't matter, there was no precedence.

So, there I was scrapping all the time and wanting to protect. One thing you'll learn about me is that in many respects I'm an utter contradiction of characters, and besides, where I came from you had to look after yourself, because if you didn't, very quickly you would be singled out and taken advantage of. Moreover, if I saw anyone taking liberties with a person weaker than themselves, I'd always get involved and fight (not always physically) for the underdog. And this is a trait that has stayed with me my entire life.

Now back to my dad... please don't think he was or is a vile man, he's a charmer and extremely funny to boot, but he is very difficult to live with and because of this, during my teens, he and I clashed more times than I care to remember, but as a young'n, behind the scenes, I was a complete and utter Daddy's Girl.

Dad has always been a great storyteller and can recall distant memories in great detail. Especially his recollections of serving in the second world war in Berlin; fighting 'The Jerries' (Germans) in bar brawls and guarding Rudolph Hess (Hitler's Deputy) in Spandau Prison. Dad remembers Rudolph Hess as a very weak mumbling man who coughed a lot. Now, as I've said, my dad was also in the Army, in a Scottish regiment called: 'The Black Watch,' he also played in the Army band as a bagpiper. So, as you can clearly see my Dad and his family got about a bit, and as a result I'm part Scottish, part Irish and English, and just to make me feel that little bit cosmopolitan there's a little bit of Spanish thrown in. What a bloody mix!

I also remember quite vividly, Dad's tales of his childhood: lots of siblings with loads of laughter; they hadn't enough money for beds for all of the children, so my dad and his brother would take it in turns: which meant fifteen minutes each on a Sunday morning to have a single bed to themselves - luxury!

My Grandma, Grannie Williamson had her boys, and one well turned out daughter too. Well, that was at least until the boys returned home covered in mud, and a whole muddy mess ensued. She was a loving and caring mum and a wonderful Grandma as well. Gran and I had a special connection, which is the reason I still miss her to this day.

Grandma Williamson (Mona) and my Grandad (Louie) were so loving and positive. My Grandad was in the Cavalry and was a fantastic horseman by all accounts. However, as a result, as he grew older, he had to have both his legs amputated. Nevertheless, having gone through such a trauma he remained full of smiles for us all, never showing the merest glimmer of bellyaching.

Eventually, they both (at separate times) ended up in the same nursing home which, as luck would have it, was close to my primary school. The two of them loved animals and we'd take our English Bull Terrier 'Bumper' along with us in the summer and wheel Granddad around the park. Granddad loved that. But suddenly, he was gone; my Grandma was distraught and suffered badly due to his absence, so unsurprisingly, it wasn't long before she ended up in the same nursing home. Fortunately for me, the home was close to my school in a village called Milton, and I'd get up early and visit her before and after school, cuddling up to her in her bed. Gran always told me that I was her favourite. She loved us all, but we had this special bond that I just cannot describe.

Her birthday is the day before mine: August the 18th (I was due earlier, but as is my way, I was late, I guess I couldn't be arsed to get out of the womb!) On a visit one day, I remember her saying to me: "Paula I think I made a big mistake coming to this place - I really miss your grandad. I love you, and I'll always be proud of you. You're my special girl." And with that she gave me an extra big hug and a kiss, this to me seemed like a subtle yet premeditated good-bye, as I remember a feeling came over me that something wasn't quite right.

The following day my dad told me that my dear Gran had passed away. And as I'd imagined my beautiful sweet Grandma must've known that that would be her very last goodbye. I was in shock, and for closure I simply had to see her with my own eyes. Up to that day, my Gran had been the only dead body I had ever seen! I remember thinking she looked 'waxy, silky, like glossed porcelain and wholly peaceful. I told her that I loved her and that I was going to achieve my dreams, then, for the very last time, I gently kissed her soft pallid face and said goodbye. I was eleven years old and truly broken hearted.

Chapter Three: The Blossoming Teen

I was always scrapping (fighting) with the lads, but due to play fighting with my brothers and them inadvertently teaching me how to punch, I very quickly learnt how to look after myself, and because of this, I would always look after the underdog. And to be honest, I would quite often win. Although one day I kicked one lad up the arse and he grabbed my leg and pulled me towards him until the skin began to come off. I remember my lip bloody killing me, nevertheless, not wanting him to think he'd hurt me I hollered: "Is that the best you've got?" While walking home crying to my mum and her saying, "What on earth have you been up to now, girl?"

I would regularly sneak out of my room, because 'unbeknown to Mum and Dad,' our house had this thing I could jump onto for a quick-fire getaway. During the first couple of years into my teens I had become a bit of a tearaway, well compared to my younger years when I was shy and got bullied. I was bullied a lot and because of this had to change schools several times. I was also abused sexually by this older girl, and one day in the playground I remember my mate, Peter punching her in the face; I remember being very grateful to him for that, and I can still visualise the moment now. My only friend was him and another boy called Brian, and to pass the time away the three of us would play He-man and She-ra in the playground. I always liked the idea of being someone else, I guess that explains my borderline personality disorder.

At the tender age of just 14 I started compiling a diary that documented my self-harm and extremely dark thoughts. Unfortunately, at that time I became extremely disagreeable towards my dad, and that was when all hell broke loose. Obviously, the little girl he once knew had all-but disappeared, and he wasn't keen on his little princess's replacement; this new-found opinionated (although always polite) adolescent that stood her ground could no longer be controlled. I was always something of a maverick … a rebel without a clue, which would give you an idea for why I was so in love with a ray of light like Madonna. Not to mention, Marilyn Monroe and Pamela Anderson from 'Baywatch' fame, who, I must admit was my first proper female crush, her, and Elizabeth Berkley, who played Jessie in the popular American series, 'Saved by the Bell'.

My bedroom paid homage to said icons, with one wall covered in Pammy posters. Right at the top overseeing the rest I had one of her naked; honoured with a sexy crimson kiss mark from my young yearning red lips. The other wall was all Madonna and East 17; I fancied Tony, who for me was the brains of the outfit. Nevertheless, I must confess, I did have a soft spot for Brian and used to go to this lad's house and watch East 17 videos whilst he and my best mate Donna kissed across the room, while I sat like a gooseberry twiddling my thumbs.

At this point in my life I was very thin, I had a broken nose, and was a late developer. Whereas Donna, had grown a massive pair of knockers, overnight. Back then I always thought I'd have to have a boob job, but soon, and to the surprise of the local boys I certainly didn't! And once I started to blossom, they just kept getting bigger and bigger! However, unfortunately they did one day cease growth, but sadly my mental difficulties didn't.

I actually developed sexually really quickly. One day I looked down and I had boobs, as if mine too had somehow grown as I slept. And with a very slim frame, long jet-black hair and a newly developed body, boys started to take more notice. My MO (modus operandi) was to play fight. I remember play fighting with this boy, it was the 4th July 1994 (I remember this well as it is American Independence Day.) Anyway, this boy threw me to the ground quite roughly and before I could fight back, I felt something warm come out of my vagina, so, immediately went home, and told my mum I'd come on my period. Today, as I cast my mind back and think of how sexually immodest I can be, I often wonder if that act of violence that, 'in some way' ,turned me on was perhaps a significant yardstick?

On the last day of school, I was technically expelled for being unruly, as I engaged in the usual antics you would expect from an overzealous teen: egg throwing, flour hurling and a cornucopia of general misdemeanours. What happened was, I arrived back late and they told me I was no longer a pupil there. Suits me just fine I remember hollering, boastfully as I ran off with the lads for more fun and frolics. So, that was that and I left school at 15! Well OK, technically I was expelled for not adhering to school rules; rules, I might add, that I deemed ridiculous. This was a bit of a shame because we were of course going to partake in the obligatory flour and egging; an act that was compulsory on your very last day of school. However, who cares, I thought, as we took ourselves off for more misadventures.

Even as a young child in my teens I always carried a bag full of pills – painkillers mainly. I hold a lot of tension in my body and would pop ibuprofen, paracetamol, and anything stronger like sweets, but strangely enough, I was against actual illegal drugs.

I did OK in my GCSEs and me and a couple of male friends went out that night on tour to find our first ever gay bar. Needless to say, we loved it. My 'Gaydar' has always been pretty spot on and through time I'd use it as a tool to seek them out and help them move on with their new sexuality. What I would do is, pretend to be their girlfriend then help them, in their own time, to 'come out' to the world refreshed and feeling alive. I used to call this converting people. Later in life, lots of these friends thanked me for my assistance. Sadly, the one I helped and was most grateful has long since died. I've lost a lot of friends and in a relatively short time, but just like I was with my Gran, unless I can see the actual body and say goodbye, I struggle to cope as the lack of closure I find incredibly difficult to cope with.

For me, school was a bit hit and miss. I adored Art and English, but really wanted to do drama. However, sadly only eight students from our whole year wanted to take it so it wasn't an option. Therefore, I created my own drama, impersonating teachers and creating my very own dinner time clubs: including one called the, 'Peg Rug Club' (seriously how old did I think I was?). The club was dedicated to making Victorian rugs out of sacks and scraps of old material. To be truthful, I only organised the clubs as a platform for me to perform and show off. I would do little sketches that I'd created, mimicking all the teachers, which obviously, the other kids championed wholeheartedly. Then came the fact that I wasn't chosen to be a pupil! How very dare they! So, an enraged moi, marched up to the Headmaster and demanded to know why? For a girl who was told almost daily to take off the heavy eyeliner and makeup and then put it straight back on again, and a girl who was always being told off for talking and distracting the other kids … was I surprised? No, not really, still, I had to stand up for what I thought was right!

Me being me, I made such a fuss that to shut me up they gave me the post of Careers Librarian: It was hilarious, I mean, who the hell was I at just fourteen years old to start advising other pupils on what careers they were fit for? Anyway, it suited me just fine, 'cos I had the keys and it also meant I didn't have to go out into the cold at dinner time. Basically, it was a farce, and my mates used to come in all the time and simply eat sweets and swing each other round on the wheelie chair singing a song I entitled: 'Do the Maude Grimes' (a Corrie Character). Mind you, this new-found position of high esteem provided me with another perfectly academic opportunity in that I quickly realised by standing on the big chairs, I could see the lad that I fancied while peering out the window; in fact two, as they were twins, but one was a little staid, so obviously I preferred the naughty one.

I would watch this boy continuously, but I would get so excited I'd throw up in the bloody bin. I've got a very obsessive personality you see; I was utterly obsessed! So, obsessed I even bought the same coat as the wayward one and would time my own departure so I could follow him part of the way home at the end of school; there would be his little crew in front and mine slightly behind.

The first time one of them spoke to me, I played it cool and barely spoke a word, but then immediately went to throw up in the bin again … how insanely attractive! Now I know I'm going on about me a lot here, but this just indicates to the reader how quickly I fall for someone, and as I've said in many interviews: "When I fall, I fall deep" and for a time I'm completely obsessed - not another soul around exists! I get utterly devoted. Oh, don't worry, the outrageous flirt in me never shuts down completely, it's just on the backburner until my infatuation has worked its way out of my bloody brain.

When we went for our GCSE results my friends' Fallows and Buckley (lads) were by my side in support. Fallows aced it: all A stars just as I knew he would. Buckley, on the other hand got sod all and said: "Oh don't worry I'll just charm myself through life!" Which he did. Those two are now the most successful businessmen our school-year has ever year churned out. Me? (I hear you say!) Oh, I did okay, I got 5 A-C's which included an A star for English (which isn't too bad for a girl who couldn't even write her name at age 9).

Now, I sensed these two were gay and I knew of course that I was bisexual, but you never spoke about it then. However, one evening I said to the two of them: "Eh, let's get dressed up tonight, celebrate and go to that gay bar in town for a laugh - take the piss and that!" See, back then, the term gay was used as an insult and they both loved the idea. I was only 15 and the second youngest in the year but I'd been drinking since I was about 13 and was reasonably proficient as a result. That night we went out and had a fantastic night! I'd love to tell you more, I'd love to tell you how we all 'came out' to each other, the crazy nights, the madness that seemed to attach itself to us, but I'm trying to focus this memoir on me and Charlie. But as this section of the book is something of a letterbox view into how Paula was built, I will just say that I helped these boys and many others 'come out' and started a crusade in support of gay rights in my own way - any homophobic comments and my 'Eccles' were well and truly up!

We had a great time exploring the scene and our sexuality and called ourselves the 'Three Musketeer's.' We were joined a little later by a very attractive lad we'd all had our eyes on at school called Colin Meredith. Incidentally, twenty years on, Colin became my housemate and is currently in my living room watching some shite reality TV whilst I type away in my dining room. Anyhow, Colin quickly became 'Dogtanian' in the outfit, and he rose to the role extremely expertly. Colin is today happy in his sexuality and is a successful and very stylish and sought-after hairdresser. You see I see things in people, attributes that most others may overlook, and I was right about Colin, who I might add has been a constant in my life, as have my lifelong friends Gareth Saldana-Fallows and Steve Buckley. The thing is with me: If you find a friend in me, you have found a friend for life.

After school came college, a place where I could finally do what I wanted, and that was Performing Arts; now I could write a whole book about our antics on that course, suffice to say they were the happiest two years of my entire life. In college I felt at home as I could finally, and totally express myself and my identity, and at weekends I'd work at 'Joe Soaps' car wash in my tiny hot pants (which looking back probably didn't look acceptable!) or perhaps I'd be in London staying with my friend in Paddington while living it up in Soho - life was wonderful! And Sam, the doorman we had come to know, would always look after us, even when I was, at times, in some right states. Unfortunately, Sam is another who is not with us anymore – God bless his soul!

In College I got to perform. I was very naughty – once hanging topless from an upstairs window to the cheering on and hoots from nearby cars – I don't know if they liked my body or were just concerned about my safety. I didn't need drink to be crazy. I'd finally met a bunch I not only felt accepted with, but I helped to run the bloody show! When it came to the performances, I'd always give it one hundred percent. And during our performance of 'Ready Steady

Go' the parents were mortified at my sexually provoking dance routines. Oh, something I forgot to mention earlier which echoes my promiscuous character somewhat: I was thrown out of Girls Brigade due to my lascivious dance moves. By now I was completely au fait with the gay scene and loved all the colourful characters that were a part of it. I also loved Geri Halliwell's carefree attitude from 'The Spice Girls', and would often mirror her look, wearing tiny, ass hugging hot pants and tights and would often wear a cartoon top.

By this time, I'd also had my first boyfriend. I met him the day he got out of the YOI (Young Offender's Institution) where he was serving time. In this boy, I saw a lost soul and because of this and many other reasons, I ventured into a loving, yet turbulent relationship with him. We lasted two years and as a sign of my devotion to him I wore his name around my neck.

It was during time I began to self-harm, this even included cutting my breasts. I was seventeen and drinking pretty heavily and would always get involved in dramas at his house. I remember once one of his mum's admirers came through the window with a sharp kitchen knife shouting that he wanted to kill us all! "Get the pan Tish?" His mum shouted. (My nickname was Tish as I looked like a little Morticia from the Adams Family) "Get the pan and twat him Tish!" She hollered again with added gusto. So, there I was alone, fighting off some big bloke who thankfully in the end relented.

This woman, my boyfriend's mum was called Gloria (she's passed now, God rest her soul). She had her own mental issues and was an alcoholic but was intuitive and clued up and knew I was self-harming. She'd been there you see and feeling my angst she helped me. The thing was I couldn't tell my own mum because she really didn't understand mental health and I didn't want it to upset her. We would often get high on aerosols, because for some stupid naïve reason I never classed this as a drug. Pfft, what an idiot! Mind you it wasn't just any old can of spray; this was Lynx Africa; we only sniffed the good stuff. Nowadays I can't smell that without immediately being thrown back to those unwise and hedonistic days. We would sit laughing and drinking for hours, and then we would go to the local pub and tell everyone what had happened. Those days were wild, but funny as hell at the same time.

Chapter Four: Lap Dancing My Way Through Drama School

Knowing how much of a loose cannon I was, my parents were never keen on me going down 'The Smoke.' But I was young and impressionable and didn't want to listen, and I'd save up and take as many trips to London to stay with friends in Paddington as was humanly possible. Our friend would sneak us into the nurse's quarters of St Mary's Hospital, and there we'd stay and party at G.A.Y, Heaven. Oh, how I loved the London scene! But at that time of life I did exactly as I wanted, a rebel heart. Mind you, I always returned home happy and unscathed.

I always knew I was bi-sexual, from a very early age, but my dad is of a different generation and not very tolerant of that kind of behaviour. Which is probably why I felt so free on the scene, I've always loved to dance and would strut my adequate stuff on the podium all night long. There were also various girls I'd kiss and under hush tones, get a bit naughty in the toilet with, 'Classy' I know, but most of us still lived with our parents so couldn't exactly take our 'promiscuous society' back there. So, it will come as no surprise that I lost my virginity at 15! Fifteen years young, on a freezing cold hill. It hurt so much…

Every relationship I found myself in was always very different from the last, because I suppose I'm a walking contradiction, and still not sure where I fit in. I think it's hard to differentiate when I'm not performing. I so desperately wanted to go to drama school in Manchester and truly study the craft. However, my teacher told me to forget it, saying that I wasn't good enough. Well I'll show you! I thought to myself. Don't ever tell me I can't do something! 'Cos I'm like a dog with a bone.

Aside from Saturdays, I didn't drink, I didn't go out with the other students; I was there to learn. After two years' or so I was desperate for some comedy, so partnered up with two friends and produced a comedy sketch for our dissertation piece. It was hard work, with long hours but was necessary in order to graduate. And, as a result I got a two one and was extremely elated.

In my final year I collapsed through exhaustion and was admitted to hospital with acute pneumonia and I almost died. I was seriously ill, and the effects of the pneumonia left me with permanent lung damage. Nevertheless, as soon as I was released from the nurses' grasp, I began filming a part and co directing for our dissertation the very next day! Comedy to me fills the soul with much needed laughter, and for me it's generally a cure for everything; even the darkest of things I sometimes turn into humour. I guess, as I learned as a teenager, it works as an immediate elixir for protecting myself.

After university came four years of me trying to get into Drama School, the one I'd picked in Manchester saw 3,000 hopefuls per year for 28 exclusive places. I was useless! Well, compared to the rest, as they'd had all the relevant training. However, unperturbed, and not one to give in to failure I simply kept on reapplying.

I'd been messing about at college hanging out of windows topless with friends holding my feet. I had to prepare two speeches, one contemporary, of which I chose, 'Educating Rita' and one Shakespeare; well I couldn't make head nor tail of what the fella was bloody talking about, and upon reading it, I was bored shitless. I'd rather drink, go out, and have a laugh.

So, it's 1997, I was working at McDonald's and met my next protégé, Grenville, who was amazing. He and I first spoke on a trip to Blackpool, which happened to fall on the day that one of my idols Princess Diana tragically died so I know the exact date; 31st August. We became amazing friends (despite him being warned off me) we travelled parts of the world together and yes, he was gay; my 'Gaydar' is spot on! More of him later but I lost him 3 years ago, and I still can't believe he's not here, he was like a bodyguard to me; a huge softie; intelligent, with so much to give, and he was funny, taken much too soon. I miss him like flowers miss the rain.

In the meantime, I worked at a cinema, and was forever in trouble; they caught me sunbathing on the roof once (see, me and Charlie love a good roof!), I nearly lost my job over it, but I wormed my way out of it. I ended up working at the cinema for ten years, travelling back from Manchester at the weekend to work there. I got one day off every fortnight as drama school was 8.30am – 6pm and I'd head straight to the library and study every day then home to my boyfriend Andy who was an adorable person and really loved and looked after me.

Andy was a gentle soul, but he liked to dabble with ecstasy. This worried me, especially after the Leah Betts story came to light, at which point I told him he'd have to pick drugs or me. Thankfully, he chose me, but he still went out, as did I, every Saturday night, so I didn't know what he was getting up to. We'd both be back up for work at the cinema every Sunday and then we'd make our drive back in the dark to our flat in Manchester.

Whilst working at a cinema I met an array of truly amazing friends who are still by my side today, one 'Stoat' (Mark) saved my life when I first overdosed. He's my rock, without him I honestly don't know where I'd be. I adore him, and Charlie sensed this, he created art for him, always asked how he was, and would often say that when he got out, he was taking him for the best meal and a few black Russians; "I need to thank him for saving my angel." Writing that just made me feel very emotional, as at the time they were the two men in my life (not-blood) who I believed truly loved me and would look after me. Well at least one of them kept that promise.

This brings me back to real time, so to conclude, I finally got a place at drama school; I said to them, "Listen I'm gonna keep coming back until I'm 60 so you either keep suffering me or give me some bloody help!" They did and within two minutes of coaching, I knew where I'd been going wrong. I got a call about a week later from Niamh the head of the school saying. "Listen we've had a big talk about you, we think you should go to London, there's a school there that just focuses on TV and we think that's the direction you should go, but if you still want to come here we are officially offering you a place." That right there was my proudest moment to date. I'd done it! I wanted to learn the trade properly, and understand once and for all, what this Willy Shakespeare was truly harping on about; thus, taking what I could of it and apply it to my trade. It was a done deal; one of which I happily accepted. With a briefing that read in my crazy head as, *'Give me half a chance, and I'll tame this bugger's shrew.'*

I was accepted by a Northern Actors Association to do another show-case; it was at this time I met another comedic close friend. The Director was a woman and I was utterly drawn to her as were the lads as well. She was stunning. After the showcase (that we'd worked on for a couple of months) had finished, I encouraged her to go to another popular destination of mine, which was Canal Street, The Gay Village. In a pub come club called Churchills one of the rougher ones, I kissed her again and again. See, I told you boys I'd get my hands on her! I was elated and took a sniff from a bullet shaped thing that some stranger offered me. I was 25 and this was my first experience of cocaine. I took more and more of this wonder drug until I felt invincible. Some close friends came back to my flat and the lady director went back to her boyfriend. My best friend Stoat knew how addictive my personality was and was upset because he knew that once I'd tried class A's I'd love them … and I did! However, it wouldn't be too long that I'd be introduced to it again in a completely different setting.

The next day I woke up and felt like a different person. I'd gone against the grain, kissed someone else and tried class A drugs. It doesn't sound much, but at that time because I was so anti-drugs it really was strange to the people around me. The sex between Andy and me had long since died; I think he loved me, and I had loved him but unfortunately I just wasn't in love with him anymore. Taking that coke had turned a page for me. I'd gone against my core values, values that for such a long time had been a part of my makeup.

Andy moved out and went back to Stoke; he did kindly helped me pay the rent for the next couple of months, but then, I was on my own. Moving back wasn't an option, besides, I love my own company. I'm never bored – I never understand when people say they are bored: Get off your arse and do some-thing then. That's when I went for an audition at a lap dancing club in Deans-gate in the City Centre. It's long since closed down now but was called 'Fantasy Bar'! I'm a person who doesn't fear things, well, nothing except for my own self, but for some reason I was absolutely terrified at that audition and hadn't a clue what I was doing. A couple of weeks before, I did go there with a friend to watch her, study her, and remember her moves, but I was so mesmerised and turned on by what she was doing in her routine and completely forgot everything she did.

Anyway, there I was about to audition for one of the owners, I was shaking uncontrollably, I was awkward getting my dress off, It wasn't too risky as we had to dance topless not naked. At the end of my audition they said I wasn't ready to work as a dancer, but said I had a good body and a pretty face, and for that reason I could work the pole. "The pole?" I asked innocently. "I can't pole dance!" "Then you'd better fucking learn, 'cos you start Friday at ten!" He replied aggressively.

Not long after, I was entrusted as a lap dancer, and went from strength to strength. To be honest, I could fill a book alone with my tales of working the club, most of which are crazy and some a little risqué. Mind you, on the dark side one thing it did reintroduce me to was cocaine; this was due to the hours being long and hard - it's not easy money like people think. I mean for a start you have to deal with a lot of bitterness and nastiness and require a thick skin to cope. A girl was crying once in the dressing room – I stormed down the stairs one time and gave the man who had upset her a piece of my mind but was immediately told off by the manager. Sometimes I was reprimanded for drinking too much … I needed it … but it was forbidden, so I used to discretely hide bottles in my bag.

A few years later The clubs also introduced me to barbiturates, diazepam to put a name to it. I needed it as I couldn't sleep. At that point I think I was about 28 and I started using more and more Benzos – basically I popped anything that ending with PAM: lorazepam, temazepam, diazepam, it's a sad and extremely irresponsible thing to admit to but I used to laugh and say that I was having a love affair with dear Pammy.

So, not being the kind of girl to waste time, I very quickly fell into the next turbulent relationship. Our nicknames were Sid and Nancy, and if you know anything about the Sex Pistols, you'll be privy to those names and iconic notoriety. This boy never touched Benzo's, but he would drink a lot and do a lot of cocaine. Our relationship was unstable, and often very physical. He got me the sack from 'Fantasy Bar' for getting into a fight with one of the punters. Anyway, that eveing I punched him so hard that night he flew off the bed and landed on the floor.

A girl I'd met that night told me to try working in Stoke, now that really was shitting on my own doorstep, however, I reluctantly rang them, auditioned, and got the job. It was a girl dancer I auditioned for, and thankfully not a pervy owner so I guess that made things a little easier. This place was different to the others I'd worked and as long as you paid your house fee, they left you alone. I was still working at the cinema, which was 10 minutes from the strip club, and as I was still in Manchester it was becoming ridiculous travelling back and forth all the time! Aside from my night antics and work, I'd got myself an agent and was auditioning a lot then getting small parts in Coronation Street, Emmerdale, Hollyoaks; I was also doing some commercials, corporate work and voice over work.

I did quite a lot of voice-over work, and also narrated a handful of books for children; I did a Roald Dahl one which was met with great feedback and was just about to go into talks to do more when I became distracted by something that was a little more up my street.

One night I'd been in Corrie and the bloke I was dancing for said "Haven't I just seen you in Coronation Street earlier?" "No … must be a lookalike!" I replied jokingly. But anyway, my cover was blown and with that everyone in the bloody club was talking about me, and from the credits they run at the end of the show they all knew my real name, as well. You see, for obvious reasons I always danced under the name Holly, and since being outed I felt a lot more vulnerable. When I adopted the role of 'Holly' I would cover myself in fake tan, put extensions in and wear false eyelashes, anything to physically transform myself. As you know, I loved dressing up and it was during my time stripping that I learnt the art of listening and watching – observation is key when you're doing something a little off-the-scale. A lot of the study is about psychology. And very quickly it becomes apparent that people walk through those doors from all walks of life, and all with a different story.

After 5 years of doing the job I had moved on from the naive person who had auditioned and was shaking like a leaf. Listen, without blowing my own trumpet, I knew I was a good erotic dancer, but had to admit that I wasn't the best looking of girls. To be honest, I wasn't the best dancer either, but I did have the best brain and knew how to shake my money-makers in just the right way; men are easy to turn on, you only have to look at some in the right way and they'll quickly throw you their weeks wages. Not long into my lap dancing tenure I was stopped working the main room, and although it had its bonuses, I actually found it a little degrading. So now the way things worked was a bit different, I would have my customers booked in at certain times and each one of them wanted something different.

One liked me to play the innocent sweet Holly, and brought me flowers to the club each week or sent them if he was away on business; this pissed some of the girls off, so, I'd always put them in water and in a safe place not in the dressing room as some of the girls were horrid and mean and would have ruined them.

A Thai girl called 'Cindy' began working and the girls were horrid to her simply because she was stunning! I befriended her and on the rare occasion when I wasn't sipping champagne in the VIP room (you don't have sex in there - apart from one occasion!) I teamed up with her – helped her and kept the other girls at bay. I did ask her if she would like to do lesbian dances with me and she happily agreed. So, what we would do is drag one or two men into the £20 room and they'd always want another dance. Lesbian dances are simulated but very saucy, and for effect Cindy was actually going down on me as I lap danced on the punter's lap and when I returned the favour, she noticed and moaned in delight. This always ensured us getting asked to do another dance. Some of the girls said she was a 'he-she', it didn't matter to me if she was or wasn't – but she was certainly post-operative that's for sure! A little while later Cindy went to take money home to her family and never came back.

Sometime after her husband came in to see 'Holly' – he said there had been some problems with her passport and she was having trouble getting back into the country, but she wanted her husband to come and see me and thank me. It would appear I was her only friend. I assumed the problem with the passport was due to her actually being a male, now I'm sorry if this is a little crude but it never tasted of anything down there, so I kind of knew. Anyway, I passed a message back to her saying I was her friend and when or indeed if she ever comes back, I looked forward to uniting again – sadly, she never did.

Many other customers liked me to be domineering, so, sometimes I'd literally come out in a cute outfit with bows and a little tartan skirt etc and say: "Get the fucking champagne … I want the best! Wait for me in the VIP area, now!" Then I'd kiss my other customer goodbye and go off and get changed into my full-on PVC fetish gear. Although tiring, it was fun playing all these characters. My suitcase (every stripper has a suitcase with various changes of clothes) was crammed full of every kind of outfit you can imagine! I started seeing a millionaire that I'd met at the club, he was such a sweetheart and utterly adored me, but then I met Emma!

I was penniless and just about making ends meet, but there was something more important on the horizon and this girl turned my head like nothing before. I told the millionaire, who was so nice and understanding about the whole situation. Before I knew it, I'd moved in with her in Stoke. I absolutely adored her, she reminded me of a (smaller) version of Shane from the L Word (My celeb crush), but Emma was real, and loved animals just like me; we had our little cat Frankie and before I knew it, we were inseparable. Emma didn't like me stripping but understood that 2-3 nights a week brought in more money than I'd earn in 2-3 weeks doing anything else. I was still doing my acting work which by now included roleplay work for the local medical school to train them up. I eventually became a facilitator and would take my own classes.

Emma and I moved into a house together (which I bought) but it was in severe need of renovation; she worked on the house relentlessly and I help stripping paper from walls in the daytime and strutted my stuff stripping clothes off through the night: goodness me it was hard work, however, the cash was rolling in and I was able to pay for everything we needed. Emma was a very proud girl, but I figured if she was doing all the work on the house it was only fair that I brought home the bacon in support of us. Finally, we were done and held a New Years' Eve party. Obviously, being one of my parties the shenanigans got out of hand and Nick (Sid!) my ex turned up and with all the noise our little Frankie (the dog) sporting his Christmas bandanna, ran off. The very next day the council rang us and said he had been found dead and they dropped our sweet little baby off in a bin bag. Opening that bag together was horrific not to mention heart breaking. We loved that little rascal so much; there was something different about Frankie, but I guess a lot of animal lovers feel exactly the same way about their much-loved pets.

Emma's mum got us a dog, Maisy, it was a little black Patterdale

Terrier. I was angry at the time because my feelings were that pets just can't be replaced, and anyway as we were still busy finishing things off the house, I felt we didn't have the time to dedicate to a new part of the family. Oh, and I'm a firm believer that you do not give a pet as a surprise present. However, it would appear that Emma's mum was only trying to help, and Maisy was, and still is the most loved dog in the world. The only downside to this little pooch was that she insisted on rolling in fox crap all the time; she'd have 3 baths a week, but I had clothes for her and even a bathrobe. She was so adorable, literally like a little baby as she drank from a baby's bottle – so cute! She'd lick her lips when she saw the bottle coming.

Anyhow, Emma and I lasted two years. During the aforementioned two years in 2011, I received a phone call from Paddy McGuinness. Apparently, Claire who I did my dissertation with had made a recording of some characters we had showcased which she secretly sent off to him a few years earlier. Back then I was alone in my flat in Didsbury and was about to eat dinner (lunch to southerners) when my agent called saying Paddy McGuiness wanted to speak with me! "Give him my number!" I yelled all over excited. The phone went down but immediately rang again. "Hello Paula, its Paddy McGuiness here!" "Alright Paddy…" I replied as if I knew him. "Listen." He said. "I was looking for a double act to support me on my tour and although I think you and Claire are hilarious, sadly I don't believe you're right for this show. However, I will keep you in mind for the future!" He'll forget us in an instant, I thought as I began miserably tucking into my food. How wrong was I? Because 3 years later I was in my office when the phone rang "Hello, its Paddy here?" came his broad Bolton accent. "Is this you Ross?" I quizzed. Ross was the boy from drama school. "No, it's Paddy McGuiness!" Anyway, it took him several minutes to convince me. "Listen, I told you I'd remember you and Claire, and I was wondering if you like to come on tour with me?" "ERM, YES!" I hollered, immediately accepting. "I'll ring Claire now and we can sort a meeting." Poor Claire, she was just about to start her teacher training, but anyway, she didn't hesitate and put it on the back burner.

We met Paddy in London and agreed to the tour. We fleshed out a couple of characters he wanted us to play and before we knew it, we were off! I learned a lot from that tour and not just about what went on stage.
After that, we were advised to go to the Edinburgh Fringe. It was a meeting we had set up in Manchester with some of Paddy's contacts, but I was insane that night, jumping from chair to chair, sitting on their laps, drinking more and more champagne. I ended up sleeping with a well-known man in the comedy circuit. In the morning I felt instant regret, left him a note, and ran. I met up with Claire and we ended up laughing our heads off. There is always a straight one to play to the crazy one and I'm sure you can guess which parts Claire and I played.

The aforementioned had come at a perfect time 'cause seven years of lap dancing had completely taken its toll - both mentally and physically. A certain hardness had come over me (self-protection) and my face looked a lot older, lines had appeared, my eyes had lost their sparkle (almost) and I knew I had to quit while I was ahead – don't be the last one lingering at the party: Leave while you're on top. Anyway, I kept having meal dates with a couple of customers, but one became obsessed with me and convinced himself that we were engaged - he was harmless enough. I had two phones of course, one for Holly and another personal one. And every now and then I would go on the odd date with these men as Holly. Emma knew all about it, I never kept anything from her. Sadly, we grew apart, physical things were non-existent, and she thought I'd become too butch –

perhaps I had?

Soon after Emma moved out, and when that door closed, I remember falling into a heap, crying, and crying until I could cry no more and said, 'Paula, pull yourself together!' And I would have to drag myself up and get myself in a good place – more mentally than physically.

Chapter Five: A Star Is Born

I always dreamt of becoming a star. A Star is born, pfft, well not quite, but hey, I did my stint treading the boards; from Stoke born Paddy McGuiness I ended up West, with Dominic in his magnificently honed role of the serial killer Fred of the same surname. This was for an amazingly written two-part drama for ITV called, 'Appropriate Adult'. It would seem a strange role for me, 'cos as I will detail later, the bullying began in attack of my supposed courting of the very character I ended up playing alongside in the aforementioned drama. That's right, I played one of the many baying paparazzi that stood in wait as the Appropriate Adult (Emily Watson) returned home to her family after her first ambivalent meet with the monster himself. Although it was a small role, I enjoyed it, and it was a step up to 'what I'd hoped would be' the big time. Dominic, Emily and the rest of the cast and crew were a dream to work alongside, and they made us all (the minions) feel extremely important.

Claire and I had to plan an original show for the Edinburgh Fringe. So, to stop ourselves from daily distractions we booked ourselves on a holiday to Turkey for 10 days to write the full show; we had a really good idea of what we wanted, and that was something along the lines of a female version of the film, The Hangover. Anyway, off we flew to Turkey with our heads overflowing with ideas. We started well as the weather was crap, forcing us to stay in and get things down. Then the next day the holiday rep came – Archie. He was German, but his family had moved to Turkey.

I have a rather sexually deviant mind and it truly takes one to know one. Archie and I immediately hit it off, whilst poor Claire sat there shaking her head. I arrange for Archie to pick us up later and take us to a nice safe bar then drop us back again. "No!" Claire said adamantly, but I insisted saying, "Look, we won't be writing anything tonight, and I fancy a drink and want to check out the bars and that." "Oh, I am not staying on my own, I'll come, but he'd better not take us off, rape us and kill us!" Claire demanded. To which I replied, "Oh don't worry dear." I was excited and looking forward to seeing him again.

A little later Archie picked us up and took us to a bar to meet some of his friends; Claire instantly took to the good looking one, but to be honest I thought the pair of them were arrogant twats! Once we'd had our drinks we got back in the car with Archie as he wanted to take the two of us for a private drink somewhere. As we navigated our way through the dark and twisting roads, Claire suddenly produced a rope and a whip that she'd found in the back of the car. "Oh God, this is it! Why the hell did I let you trick me into this?" She yelled.

At this point, and due to her nervousness I asked Archie to drop her off, but for some reason she stayed with us and a few minutes later we arrived at a lovely house, entered, and our esteemed host Archie poured each of us a glass of wine. Claire being terrified pretended to drink her wine, which was a shame 'cause if she had have drank a little, it probably would've calmed her down. And due to the lack of nerve reducing alcohol one of the photos she had taken came out so blurry as she was shaking like a bloody leaf. I didn't want to put her in this situation, but I simply found Archie utterly fascinating. We had many things in common and spoke a lot about World War 2, highlighting stuff that a great many of the German people I've met over the years seem reluctant to talk about. I told him we had his whip and immediately, he called me master! We then gave him our 'Brides of Comedy' business cards to put up on his wall, and then I instructed him to take us back to the hotel – "A Master demands its slave." I told him. "Yes master." He replied, and off we went. "Yes Claire, I told you he might be a bit odd, but I also told you that we wouldn't get raped and killed!" I whispered in Claire's ear. Nevertheless, Claire was still a nervous wreck: well, she was at least until she had a brandy and found the funny side of it.

In the day we wrote the show, or should I say just sat there creating characters while filming ourselves. Once we were in character, we'd remain in them until we felt that we couldn't hold in the laughter anymore! But we would always be full on; I suppose people in the know would class us as method actors in that sense. The following night, after shopping for suitable shoes we met Archie again, poor Claire wasn't happy. This time I took the whip to him, and as I humiliated and picked on him, Claire sat alone on the sofa, downstairs. This went on forever, as we were both in our perfect roles. No sex! No intercourse of any sort! Listen, to ask a dominatrix for sex is unacceptable … faux pax! It's just never part of a dominatrix's briefing!

The following day Archie had to go to work, he left me a message re what time he would be back, and I was now alone because Claire had taken a taxi home. So, I climbed out onto the roof and enjoyed the rays of the sun while filming myself saying how liberated I felt on the roof with miles and miles of nothingness in front of me. Simply me and my wonderfully playful, sometimes dark, thoughts. Mind you, sadly the video I made that day went missing a year later when my laptop was stolen, and Claire was less than pleased because we'd lost valuable time. I apologised and told her not to worry because I would come up with more material that was even better later that evening – and I did. (However, I'm almost positive Claire had that footage as well.) I laughed so much that night, I almost wet myself (where on earth was Archie when I needed him).

Anyway, we spent the rest of the holiday writing, but I told Archie that we needed to find a friend to bring along that would be suitable for Claire and fortunately he brought home the bacon, in the form of the perfect man, Riddick! I told Archie that we should all go to the beach, and that I would like a little dog to come along too. So, he picked up a friend's dog, and we picnicked and played with the dog, then we swam and chatted about the future. Strangely, our time spent that day reminded me of the '50s: film-noir-esque yet with colour added. The trip ended with me saying that after our trip up to Edinburgh, we'd return.

Well, our trip up to sunny Scotland went exceedingly well, with our show to my delight being reviewed as, and I quote: 'The crudest show to have ever hit, the fringe!' Claire however, met this review with severe distaste. But we'll agree to disagree on that, because I myself hoped the show would come across racy and raunchy, my homage to the American box office smash, The Hangover, which was marmite to the audiences, as it was both loved and hated in equal measure. Oh, and I met a wonderful bunch of Aussies (Australians) into the bargain. We ended our month run absolutely exhausted, but immediately booked a trip to Turkey.

It was around this time I developed an eating disorder, bulimia, and due to this, my weight plummeted to a devastating seven stone and in a fit of self-loathing I swallowed every single tablet I could put my hands on. My friends Stoat and Claire who were always there in what I referred to as my 'hazed state' called for an ambulance and I was immediately seen by a psychiatric team known as RAID, they suggested I be admitted, and I happily agreed. I was extremely happy about this because I knew that if I was allowed home, the stash of pills I'd hidden would lead to me taking an overdose once again. And also, at this point, Deviant, my so called friend entered on a quest to turn my friends against me, which kick-started my relationship with debilitating suicidal thoughts that very soon escalated to actions.

Anyway, it was time to leave, and on my exit, my friend Stoat (forever by my side in support) and I shot straight up to London to meet one of my dearest friends, and on our arrival, we drank until we dropped – we drank until the wheels came off. I remember visiting the home of one of our finest writers, Charles Dickens and I also remember how good it felt to eat from real dinnerware, with proper stainless-steel cutlery again instead of the plastic I had very quickly become accustomed to while in psychotherapy. We had a fantastic trip, but it was time to return home; so, I'm Manchester bound.

Once home, I started sessions with a counsellor, and was back to work in Manchester, trying my upmost to get my life back to some normality, still all the time, struggling. I was on a mixture of medications, and life was hard, but hey, I had bills to pay. Fast-forward ten years to yet another surprise waiting just around the corner for me. When, on my arrival home from work one day I found a letter strewn across my hallway-carpet-runner, with a biro-doodled spider dangling haphazardly from the capital of my Christian name. Who the hell is this from? I wracked my brain. Until a split second later, it dawned on me, and like a shaft of rhapsodic light through my eager brain it came: It's Charlie – my word, the man has actually taken the time to reply to me...

Chapter Six: Introduction To The Twins

While writing back-and-forth, Charlie somehow managed to get me hooked on everything to do with the Kray twins; how he spoke about them was simply beguiling. And, after a great deal of research into them and their ilk my interest soared and the very idea that they were proper old school Londoners, really appealed to me, and the added bonus was that their 'manor' (as many Cockney's referred to it) was the East End which had me totally intrigued. There is something about the East End of London that somehow seems familiar to me, because I feel they possess similar values to us northern folk: spoken of course with intonation reminiscent of Jane McDonald.

As it 'appens, I was reasonably accustomed to London and its way of life, because I had been visiting there for many years, back as far as my inno-cent teens. I often travelled down there with friends and would always shoehorn in a trip to the 'Ten Bells Pub' on Commercial Street, for this is one of the only remaining boozers that date back to the eery Jack The Ripper era, 1888. And for some reason, I have been forever drawn to his final victim, Mary Jane Kelly. So, every time I'm in Leytonstone, London I like to visit and take flowers to tidy up her grave a little. I also have her name, tattooed about my person, alongside a catholic cross; I sound like a bit of a lunatic – and I s'pose I am a bit.

But why am I drawn to her? I hear you ask. Well, I guess it's because I believe in all of that stuff, past lives etc, much to the point that I have been hyp-notised and while under I regressed back to that exact time. I also hold a deep hankering to ensure that these kinds of negatively iconic women are somehow remembered, moreover, Mary Jane Kelly is a beacon for the many sex workers through history who faced abuse, violence, and rape, especially those who were subsequently murdered as a result. Unfortunately, as a need to feed themselves and their kith and kin, to the female of the species prostitution is one of the oldest professions, and sadly today the same truth remains. And among many up and down the UK, Commercial Street still has working girls braving the cob-bles 'to earn a bob' every single night. I have extremely strong views regarding prostitution; I have always felt an affinity with sex workers, well at least they are open and honest, it's the women who marry purely for money who are the kind of prostitute I have no respect for. And I'd take honesty over women who live a lie, any day of the week.

While in London, I visited the Blind Beggar, and took along my gay friend for some support, passing him off as James 'The Job', just to see if it started any tongues wagging. This was my first time to the Beggar and I didn't know a soul. As I entered the notoriously-iconic establishment I was picked up by the 'Yellow-Pages' of great British crime, Dave Courtney; to be honest, at that point I had no idea who the hell he was, and even less idea that in a few years to come he would be the best man making a speech at my wedding. It was here were I first met Charlie's son Michael. Michael was a real gentleman to me and nothing like I'd expected. I then met up with Nicole, and after a quick kiss with a well-known 'face' from the British gangland fraternity, she came back to my hotel with me. This was all a bit strange, and I very quickly learned that she was in fact gay; more importantly, married.

I was also introduced to a most eccentric looking man known as, Toby Von Judge; the night was surreal and real, and opened up a whole new world of intriguing people to me, which, over a very short period of time, grew and grew. Around this time I had a bit of an on-off relationship with a bloke called Michael Coleman, this lasted for about 12 months, and for the most part he treated me well, that was unless we had a little disagreement, in which case he would quickly turn from Jekyll to Hyde. Michael came from a tremendously wealthy and loving family; I had never been around people with such wealth, but they welcomed me in graciously and for a period of time I felt accepted. However, Michael had a particular taste, one such oddity was having an overabundance of fruit machines in his house. Nevertheless, the main thing was he did have a wonderful sense of humour, and at times we definitely saw a future for us together. But as always seems the case, in the end I didn't quite fit in; he was forever judging how much I drank, and this negative opinion thrown my way simply bolstered my need for even more alcohol.

We visited the Kray graves and Frances Shea's (Kray) too. I made friends with her niece, also called Frances Shea. Fran and I clicked immediately, she suffered from mental illness too, and this, for the two of us, proved to be great support. For some unknown reason, there was one male individual who worshipped the Krays, yet slagged off Fran. I would always stick up for Fran despite her heavy protest insisting that she didn't need sticking up for; but I would have done the same for anybody. The way this man and this Facebook group were cyber bullying her was utterly disgraceful; little did I know what was around the corner, heading my way from the same wrongdoers.

Recently, I had been back and forth through the mental health care system and been given the diagnosis, borderline personality disorder, which I must admit, for them to come to such a decision after observing the signs I was showing was absolutely spot on. Moreover, finally, there was diagnosis and a name for what I felt was simply me 'going mad.' And for that reason alone, I found that the diagnoses came as a great help. I was immediately put on certain meds, (medication) which unfortunately made me feel like a zombie; It took over me, I felt out of control and couldn't get a thing done. So, in the end I ditched the prescription meds because they offered no alternative. And to this day I believe this BPD has led me down some extremely rocky roads.

Every time there was a get together at the Blind Beggar I would be there, making more and more friends and acquaintances week-on-week. One person who did make me laugh was Bev Straker, however, she didn't like Michael one bit. Toby Von Judge was a well-documented eccentric man, who claimed to have known or knew everybody, and indeed, many circulated photos were testimony to this. Nevertheless, no matter what the reality I loved the man,

'Grandpops' as he liked me to call him, and I loved him for that, too. Not to mention everything else he was about, his eccentricities and choice of off-the-wall, yet stylish attire had me wholly captivated. The way he kissed a certain ring on his finger, had me in fits of laughter. Sadly, one night after a get together at the Blind Beggar, while Michael was driving Toby home they had an almighty row and never spoke again, this left me in a very awkward situation because obviously Toby still wanted (much to Michael's anger) to see me, so I would go and stop at his place if I felt he really needed me around.

Chapter Seven: Handlebar Moustache and a Dream

January 2016 came, and I was hit by an artic lorry. Then, eight days later I took a huge overdose! In my daze I managed to drag myself to the top of stairs, then passed out and fell all the way down and was apparently laid unconscious for over twelve hours. Stoat called my mum, and they instantly came round to my house, but because I was slumped at the bottom of the stairs, right by the door, the two of them struggled to get in. Apparently, there was blood everywhere, with the faintest pulse, and due to the horrific scene in front of them, Mum called for an ambulance. Dad was there too but all he was worried about was the cats, never mind me laid on the bloody floor dying. Once they got me to the hospital they immediately began resuscitating me, apparently, I was slipping away. According to the medics and doctors, if they hadn't seen to me when they did, I may not be here writing these notes.

Eventually, I came round, and I was furious and started ripping out the IVs in my arm etc; I had to be restrained and was kept in while being monitored for four days. By this time, I was in a rather strange mood, I put a bedpan on my head and said I was off to London, then got out of bed and fell over, revealing my posterior to everyone in a ten-yard radius. After this little episode, and for a while after, Mum and Stoat stayed with me – simply to keep me in check. I was extremely upset and felt that I didn't want to be alive anymore, I'd had enough of being a burden to everyone, and tried another suicide attempt; at the time it seemed the only vocation open to me. Nevertheless, it would appear that I am bloody rubbish at it, hence the many failed attempts. Well, either that or I'm bloody invincible … there can be no other explanation.

Charlie was horrified at the news and wrote me a long letter saying he was there for me and that I had such a lot to offer the world. I obviously took his words on board, but they can't have made much impact because soon after, while over the limit on drink, I tried crashing my car and was nicked – so, yet another failed attempt. Soon after my physical recovery, I was back auditioning and filming, although due to my not being able to drive, it was proving to be something of a logistical nightmare. However, that same year I tried focusing on getting physically and mentally well; I threw myself into work whether that was, teaching or taking on certain roles as a jobbing actor.

For me, escapism is what it's all about, not being Paula for a while and changing myself into different characters; I'm forever making characters up in my head and while doing mundane jobs (e.g. washing dishes etc) I'd be talking to myself making out I was in some sort of documentary. See, I told you I was bloody crackers! I did a full day just for fun dressing as different characters: we dressed in full and I did everyone's make up. Charlie loved parts of how I lived my life, he said there was never a boring element whatsoever, and he also said that that part of my character was what initially drew him to me. And, in a similar way this was what originally drew me to him. Charlie could often be found wearing a different mask and this along with his overt sense of survival (notice-able from the humour in his art) was why I gravitated towards him.

Throughout the next year our bond grew stronger and at this point he asked me if I would like to visit him.

Before being cleared as one of his main visitors I had to go through a multitude of rigorous checks. During the time of getting approved a great deal of important things seemed to go missing, and it took months and months for me to get the actual clearance to visit. However, a little while later the go-ahead I'd been hoping for finally came through, and a date for my first visit was set for the 11th November; I remember the date distinctly because the following day was Remembrance Sunday, and coming from a military background, memories from a young age hearing the bugle call were etched in my forever memory.

I was very excited to finally have a date set and had already put in place that I would make my first visit along with a man called Basky, a man who I had already met having borrowed a Charlie banner from him some time earlier. I was desperate for that banner to be seen all over the world by Charlie's supporters, so I took it with me on a trip to Portugal with Stoat. For the initial meet, Charlie had stressed that he wanted me in black; it took me a while to find 'the-one', but I finally decided on a black tight dress with a zip up the front, black tights and black stiletto heels, oh, and a full-length black coat that fanned out at the sides. So, it's the day of the meet, and at this point for the readers pleasure Lee insists we get a little theatrical. *So here goes.*

Poised in the prison wings I heard the jangle of the jailer's key-fobs and chains, while a distant echoed hum of a thousand prisoners' voices mur-mured an air of menace up and down the corridors. And as my nerves fraught yet not visually apparent edged ever closer to the surface, we stood and waited patiently in the reception area of the infamous sixteenth-century prison, as I fought with all my might to quell the eruption of fear from making an uninvited appearance.

While taking a second to catch my breath, a brace of smart, yet awk-wardly dressed officers appeared and shepherded us along, making our way through the main prison and on to a set of bleak and unnerving wrought-iron gates, and out onto an insipid grey and wet concrete yard. Then, in a moment of deafening silence came the sound of the heavy doors as they locked behind us, and momentarily, a feeling of claustrophobia and immediate apprehension enveloped me. At which point I turned to our mutual friend Basky.

Now this man Basky is no slouch: he's a thickset and heavily tattooed man, bold and brash, who wears an instantly recognisable tattoo, the tattoo of the notorious and infamous man that Basky and I are seconds away from meet-ing. The man, our esteemed host, dubbed 'Britain's most violent prisoner' is about to come out from the shadows, as Basky, with hands all a-tremble stands holding a tray of food, while his entire body is shaking in anxious doubt, doubt of not knowing exactly what lurks behind the security of the shadows.

Up until this point, I had been as cool as a cucumber, yet the two-and-a-half-hour journey to the bleak 'Cat A' mens prison had passed quickly as we chatted the time away wondering what our friend who had up until now only existed on paper was going to be like in the flesh. A reality that we were soon going to realise on our arrival to the 'Big House,' an institution better known among the tabloids and criminal fraternity as: 'Monster Mansion'!

I had been writing to him for the past three years and sharing many of my personal feelings with him over that time. Our gradual and casual correspondence had quickly turned into a friendship, and over the past nine months or so there were hints of much more. In our letters, a cheeky tone had begun to show its face, and a flirtatious scattering of kisses graced the pages, instead of the simple impersonal monikers. The man I was about to meet had released me from the darkest corners of my past. And in its place presented me with a light, serene and tranquil existence, cemented with his compassionate, ever supportive words shared through notes passed and his non-stop humour had me laughing again, which up until our union had become an unattainable memory.

Despite being thirty-two years my senior and having spent forty-three years in prison; thirty-eight of those years languishing in solitary due to his violent and volatile behaviour towards staff members and inmates alike. This man seemed to understand the core of me, allowing me to share my innermost thoughts freely with him without fear of embarrassment. This, in turn, opened the door and let free my dark sense of self-deprecating humour, allowing it to flow out onto the paper of which I wrote to him.

During our three years writing and sharing many photos with one another, a Valentine's card was sent rather titillating, albeit in a funny way. The card, I was sure would be tossed into a pile marked for the rubbish, along with a whole heap of others sent from other likeminded women that are drawn to a man with Charlie's elite set of credentials; a type which funnily enough I had never classed myself in the same vein as.

Basky, the usual confident hard man of brawn and muscle was still clearly nervous, he was tucked in close to my side fumbling and tripping up over his own words, not quite sure what to say when our prestigious penfriend surfaced. "Oh, it'll be fine." I assured him while struggling to fix my tights; upon the realisation that I had been gifted with a dirty great ladder right down one side of my carefully selected black 10 denier; a choice that seemed befitting for such a monumental and challenging occasion. "Oh, look at my bloody tights?" I gasped! "Bloody hell! I look a right bloody mess. What a fucking farce!"
"I don't think it's your tights he's gonna be looking at Paula!" replied the husky voice of Basky as he gave a cheeky wink and a smile, shaking his head at the fact that the tight, cleavage revealing zip-up black dress I was wearing was a little low cut for such a prison engagement.
"Well!" I joked. "I must give the poor sod something to look at, mustn't I? He's been banged up all day every day for a bloody lifetime!" Nonetheless, as soon

as he had uttered the words did the doubt at my choice of outfit rear its ugly head, as my brain evoked images of black skinny jeans and a chiffon shirt, in homage to an alternative option that may have been a little more appropriate. However, it was too late now, as we neared another set of giant barred doors that led down a little concrete slope, "Watch your step Miss?" said the guard ever so politely. And he was right, because the ground was indeed very slippery and true to form, I lost my balance and went arse over tit almost crashing into the poor unsuspecting guard. Fortunately, I managed to grab onto the wall, and regained some composure.

"Chop, chop boys … shall we move along?" I skittishly insisted, in the hope of concealing any hint of embarrassment as we moved on to yet another set of doors, and as soon as the key turned in the lock I heard a gruff Cockney voice ghoulishly whisper from somewhere close by: 'B-a-s-k-y! P-a-u-l-a! Is that you? Where have you been? Pauuuulllllaaa! Basssskky! Cam on!'

At this point, my stomach turned somersaults, like a car trying to start on a cold winters day. And in that moment my 'comic book' thoughts become a reality, for now it was my turn to got to war with my nerves. I turned to Basky (who was behind me still holding the tray of food) and quickly the words escaped my lips, "Oh my God! Shit! We are really going to meet him. I am bloody nervous as hell now Basky … are you?" But the ashen pallor that took-over his rugged face had long before given the answer I was expecting, as he mumbled, "Yeh! Too right I am girl."
With that, the door momentarily swung open but immediately closed behind us - and we were in there all alone, as the guard had gone into the adjoining room.

Over in the corner of our isolated room was a man of fine muscular build, with a bit of white stubble on his face, wearing a vest and tracksuit trousers, darting from one foot to the other on the spot as he danced with his fists up sparring as if ready to go into battle in a boxing ring. His green eyes flashed an amalgam of hunger and excitement, those steely eyes burning as if a fire was behind them, yet on his face he wore a cheeky smile, with a strangely inviting stare. And with Basky frozen to the spot behind me, I glanced over provocatively and said "Come here Charlie … it's me!" Which he did, and I gave him a huge endearing hug.

In that moment, that split-second moment as our eyes met, and our souls were entwined an image burned itself into my psyche. This was an extremely provoking image that made it clear to me that I had just met the most infamous British prisoner of all time, Michael Gordon Peterson – more infamously known as, Charlie Bronson.

The meet was far more enjoyable than I'd initially imagined; I had conjured up scenes of a rather delicate engagement, full of extremely nervous pauses and fleeting embarrassing exchanges. 'Well, not on your nelly!' Because you see, within no time at all Charlie and I were dancing round the room to football results. Yes that's right, bloody footy results! Well, we hardy had a choice of music, now did we. I scanned the room for a second and found Basky sat like a third wheel across the room from us. I caught his eye momentarily, and he was giggling and shaking in wonder. Charlie and I spoke about everything and nothing, and his cheeky flirtatious quips came thick, fast and inviting, and given half a chance he would have… well, I'm sure you can fill in the gaps. Then came the kiss; a kiss that would hopefully seal the deal. You see, for a woman like me that first kiss is very much a 'do or die' kind of moment, and in that transitory moment, *boy did I live!*

At times in the meet I had to give myself a reality check, simply due to the bizarre nature of the situation. No sooner had we left Charlie did Basky make a prediction, stating: "You are going to marry him." To which I quite adamantly replied: "Don't be so bloody ridiculous! I will probably never see him again!" Nevertheless, it was difficult for me to keep concealed the fact that my stomach was doing somersaults, backflips and all-sorts. We contemplated stopping on the way home so that I could punch Basky in the eye and make up a story that Charlie had given him a friendly right hook; obviously we didn't go through with it, apart from which the news of such to the prison hierarchy would have done him no good whatsoever.

When I got home that evening, I immediately sat at my desk and wrote Charlie a letter. Then, first thing the next day, I posted it so that he would get it on the Tuesday. Charlie must have had the same thought, because that very same day I received a letter from him, too.

Strangely enough, our letters were almost identical. In his letter he asked if I would like to receive phone calls from him, and if so, he would need my number; at which point he would remove someone else from his allowed call list – he's only permitted to have ten numbers. Charlie also asked me to get a landline with a recording device so that it would be cheaper, and we could also spend a lot more time on the phone. So, I went into town and got one, and, true to his word, first thing at 8.30am that Saturday morning, a call came in. Obviously, he had made me aware of the time to expect his call, but what I didn't expect was how long we would be on the bloody blower – an hour and half of non-stop chat. From that day forward, every Sunday morning was the same, his call would come in, we'd have our ridiculously lengthy chat and I would come off the phone feeling the highest of highs imaginable. Charlie would also call on a Wednesday afternoon, but if I was working, he would leave me a beautifully sweet and uplifting message.

Christmas came, and someone from that Facebook bully-boy group suggested that we do a Christmas calendar for Charlie. This 'I might add' was the same credulous tosser who had slagged off my friend Frances Shea – but, eh, I'll get to him a little later. Anyway, everyone in Facebook-land now knew of our close friendship and using my PayPal account we did a whip round, and with my £200 contribution it came to £500. I immediately informed Charlie that every single one of his supporters had chipped in - Charlie was very touched. I visited as close as I could to Christmas and cut out loads of pictures of him and did a Christmas tree, hanging pictures of Charlie, me and a load of our friends on it, it was a very full and fun tree.

Chapter Eight: Charlie's Right Hand Woman

Towards the end of January 2017 Charlie said "What if I wanted to get out and make a life with you?" It was obvious that our relationship was now that of partners, but I had to be clear and asked him how he saw me? Moreover, where our relationship was heading. Cutting me off to put his point across Charlie jumped in and said: "You're my fackin' soulmate babe. I wanna life with you … 'cos with you, sweetheart, I dare to imagine a future … well, if you want one with me?" And in much the same way that he had jumped in to answer to my initial question, I did the exact same, and said: "Well of course I bloody do, I'm utterly in love with you, and yes, you are my soulmate, too!"

With that, and somewhat out of the blue he happened to mention the idea of proposing to me on Valentine's Day. I chastised him saying it seemed a little obvious! I said this knowing Charlie wouldn't want to make a mug of himself in case I refused. Anyway, after this call it was clear to see that the two of us wanted from life what other couples eventually long for. Especially given the time, and I mean 'quality time' Charlie and I had truly spent with one another over the past three years. Let's face it, through letters and meets we only had our relationship to talk about. Moreover, a prison relationship is free from the kinds of distractions that most 'civvy' couples have to deal with in their relationship's infancy.

I had obviously confided in my close friends and felt that it was now time to tell my parents. Well as I expected, initially Mum was horrified, and my dad's opening words were: "Well if nothing else, he's a bloody good fighter!" Anyway, as the news spread a little, Charlie and I knew that the news would leak out to paparazzi land almost bloody instantly, and that before many hours had passed, someone somewhere would be selling the story. Charlie had enough experience of this, so he told me to do a 'pre-emptive strike' and get in touch with the tabloids myself; he expressed to me that this way we would at least have a certain level of control.

I didn't have a clue what I was doing, but I called and spoke to several newspapers, and was tentatively giving them the minutest of details, but as I'm sure you know, journalists have a very good knack of sifting information out of you. Anyway, in the end I decided to settle with The Daily Mirror, simply because I got on well with Gemma, one of their employees.

While in the process of sorting out the media, I was on a job, and had to keep running out to the car every now and again. I was in Bolton at the time doing a job for a company I'd already done work for in the past, anyway they'd booked me in at a police training centre in Wakefield, which coincidentally, was not too far from the prison. So, I spoke to the head of the company to let him know what was going on, and also stated to him that I understood if due to my link up with Charlie they wanted to have me replaced. However, surprisingly he said it would be perfectly ok, but showed a little concern for why I would want to be with someone with such a notorious reputation. I told him, as I told others, that I wanted to be with him in spite of his infamy, and that there was more to Charlie Salvador than was reported in the press. I was extremely happy in the knowledge that despite all of this criminal baggage my work would not be affected.

Recently, I had been sent to Germany to perform and represent Monohulled Medical School in a worldwide medical communications training conference, and was helping them re-write part of their curriculum, in the capacity of an actor, role-player and facilitator. Anyway, I was contacted that night by the boss I had been working for in Bolton; it was obvious that he had googled Charlie and I was told to cancel all work I had scheduled for them including the police job. To be honest, I wasn't at all surprised and told him I was sorry that I would now have to be replaced. Naively, I had the idea that there might be a bit of a lull in work, but honestly thought it would pick back up once everything had died down. To be honest, I really didn't expect the knock-on effect collateral damage that came later.. However, looking back, I can't believe I was that stupid.

The Mirror newspaper was quick to take over and immediately a contract was sent over with a motorcycle courier for me to sign. I went through it, but because the rider was waiting to take it back, I very quickly scanned through it. As is always the case with the 'nationals', which is something I've learnt over time, the actual contract was a little more extensive in its requirements than was mentioned in our phone chat, stating quite emphatically that they wanted far more than we had originally agreed, so inevitably, once I'd signed in haste on the dotted, I was totally screwed. Remember this was my first dealing with the press.

Charlie expected me to get something around £10k, because apparently that's what his previous wife, Saira got; my figure was nowhere near this, the tabloids don't pay anything near what they used to, not with the internet, and people walking round with a mobile film crew under the hood of their iPhone (other manufacturers are of course available). I tried to explain this to Charlie but due to the way his life is behind the veils of incarceration he simply doesn't understand change. And I guess for the time he's living under the pleasure of her Maj, he never will - it's completely understandable.

The Mirror of course, acted very astute in their approach, and during their phone call, they managed to convince me that they had the full pictorial, voice and filming rights of the proposal. Moreover, they stated that I was to stay in hiding, as best I could, until the 13th of February when they would take my friend Colin and me up to Wakefield. When that day arrived, we took the trip up on the train and they put us up in a hotel for the night. We met briefly with their people and arranged a time for a meet sometime the next morning. Colin, a hairdresser by trade was doing my hair; I had already decided to wear a red dress, which was handy because they'd advised me not to wear black! To compliment the dress, I chose to wear mauve stilettos, and due to the cold and dismal Yorkshire weather, I would don a full-length black coat.

The night before Colin and I tried to find a gay bar - we very quickly found one; it was a bit of a dive, but I didn't care, as it was my final night out before the next day's events unfolded. The two of us were desperate to get on the dancefloor, but instead, got chatting to some lads at the bar. During the conversation, somehow it slipped out that I was here to accept Charlie Salvador's proposal of marriage; and due to our naivety thought nothing of it. I could have parked a ten-ton-truck in Colin's mouth for opening his trap. Nevertheless, the lad didn't believe it anyway, which we found extremely funny and we mocked and joked about it for a good time after. I was bloody glad I had Colin with me, it made me feel more secure.

Once back at my hotel feeling happy and uplifted I took a shower, and made the epic fail of leaving all of my makeup on, and as the water ran down me it smudged my mascara, I got out of the shower and gazed deep into the mirror, at which point I began to cry; subconsciously, I think it had suddenly dawned on me that I may have bitten off more than I could chew, and thought perhaps the proposal should have remained private, but it was Charlie's idea to get the tabloids involved. Charlie was on the ball with this sort of stuff and had said that we should sort it before someone else cashes in on it, in which case we would end up with sweet F.A (fuck-all). Furthermore, if that had happened, we would have ended up having no control whatsoever over what was written. Thankfully, due to Charlie's clued-up approach, I had insisted on a copy of approval from Gemma and the paper, so everything was in our hands and could never be contested.

Promptly, as the hotel clock struck a single chime for 10.00am, in walked Gemma with a photographer and filmmaker in tow. (Turns out it's a photographer who knew my best friend from years back). Anyway, they were both very charming and asked if they could film while I had my hair done, and for some reason they wanted to catch me as I applied my shocking red lipstick in the mirror; looking back, I bloody hated this footage, it made me look like a pissing tart. Unfortunately, at that point in the day I was riding the crest of the wave of excitement, and for me, getting all made up for Charlie was one of the highlights of the day.

The crew recorded masses of stuff, but once edited, as I originally thought, I felt I came across tarty, and regrettably so did several close friends. I remember thinking, If this is to be the only footage the nation sees, if they hadn't made their minds up about me already, then this piece of film would truly seal the negative deal.

In addition to all-of-the-above there was the car parked suspiciously across from the prison, which was obviously paparazzi; so, while my mind was flooded with all of this crap, I was trying to divert myself back to all the messages I needed to pass on to Charlie. Not to mention the fact that the Mirror had said that in the event of a rival paper getting any shots of me the deal would be terminated, which as you can imagine was something that kept overtaking my already anxious brain as a warning. Having said that, they still wouldn't be getting the exclusive interview with Charlie the next day, and as Charlie had said, it takes one screw to tip the press off, so no way could that be my fault.

Anyway, we did what we did, and the Mirror got what they needed. In the pics from the Mirror I was taking huge strides because I was told to get there quickly, so to anybody viewing the pic's I simply look as though I daren't step on the cracks in the pavement. Plus, my dress which actually came to just above the knee kept rising up and up so you could almost see what I had for dinner, which was nothing as I could never eat a thing before a visit; I was bloody mortified.

The visit went well, Charlie loves me in red, and once we got his business messages out of way, it was time to get serious, mind you, I had to prompt the forgetful bugger, but, after a right-hook, to his jaw he proposed on bended knee and said: "I've never met anybody in my life like you. And there is nobody I would want to have a life with more than you. I love you Paula, you are my soulmate, will you marry me?" To which I replied rather cheekily, "Of course I will, now get up off that floor or you will do yourself an injury, a man of your age!" At which point we kissed, and he shouted our announcement for others on the segregation wing to hear, and they cheered raucously in acknowledge-ment. He then shouted it to the officer on duty and she congratulated us; we were both elated, and nothing could break that. I was safe, loved and wanted again. It was Me and Charlie against the world, and oh boy, we were going to show 'em.

On that day, Charlie and I made a pact, and part of that pact was that I would do everything in my power on the outside to support his hope of progres-sion, as long as he did everything he could on the inside to protect himself. We shook hands and kissed to seal the deal, and for my part of the deal I would never go back on my word. By now it was time to leave. I was immediately ushered out with the rest of the visitors, but with complete butterflies; I tried hard to conceal my massive smile but couldn't. The car from the Mirror was parked in waiting outside. Somebody, I haven't a clue who, hustled me into the backseats, and Colin immediately threw a blanket over my head.

As you would imagine, The Sun's 'paps' were on high alert, and be-cause of this a high speed car chase evolved, this was great fun, I didn't want it to end, however, as soon as we had lost them we picked up my things, made our way to a private location where they conducted a short interview, then it was back to my house to reflect on the day.

Charlie and I had said that we wanted lots there for the call that he was going to make but the Mirror forbade it; one friend only was allowed, and Robbie who was going to be my bridesmaid, but even when she arrived she was told she had to leave. And yet again came the fear, when I was told that if Charlie didn't call, any deal would be down the pan. I tried my best to explain the obvious to them, that he was in prison on the segregation wing and couldn't just call us when he fancied it – it had to be formally arranged through the right channels.

Charlie had given me a time slot, a makeup lady put my face on, and I had all my house rearranged due to lighting, and then we simply waited and eventually the call came in. And as I lifted the receiver, we could hear Charlie singing, Frank Sinatra's 'My Way', with a slight air of artistic license as my soon to be husband changed the main lyric to 'Our Way'. Mind you, I will just admit that because I was so nervous, when his first call came in, I pressed the wrong bloody button for the loudspeaker and cut him off by mistake. However, after the initial mishap the phone rang again, Charlie made the proposal and I very happily accepted.

I was so excited and happy I completely forgot that the cameras were there, but I was immediately jolted back to reality when I was given a box with mine and Charlie's faces on the front (which I imagine was an idea of Rod's) and inside was a beautiful diamond engagement ring; anyway, that was that, the day had finally arrived - I was engaged. After which we moved into the garden where they did some shots of me wearing the ring; then we had some prosecco and pizza and a toast was made to me and my new Fiancé.

The next thing on the agenda was an interview; I very quickly decided to go for it big time and take on Piers Morgan, simply because I believed that interview would be the most thought provoking, if not simply provoking. The next day the Daily Mail, Mail on Sunday and some female journalist came to interview me, and again, I had my hair and make-up done because they had sent a photographer. It was extremely exciting, although, I did feel a bit silly saying certain things, because we all know how judgemental people can be, but I wanted Charlie to enjoy the article, too.

That weekend it was all over the papers. The Sun had got a sneaky shot of me and had even zoomed in on the Salvador necklace I began to wear. My mum didn't want to talk about it, she was worried to death, journalists had found my family and where they all lived, one of my brothers is a copper so I was worried for him, but he was OK and said "As long as you are happy", but these words were few and far between.

It was now fully out, Gemma kept calling to say who called in and my home phone was ringing off-the-hook with journalists from across the globe. By now though, a deal with GMB had been struck up; however, in haste, due to all the excitement I didn't prepare totally myself for the reality of what was to unfold. So that was that, GMB, my first live interview to date, and who do I choose for a sparring partner? Yeh, you got it, Piers 'I'll have the last word' Morgan, mind you that's me all the way, jump in feet first without a care for the consequences.

In truth, my idea was thus: If I could handle him, I could handle anyone. As the interview began, he immediately started to give me a hard time; but because I was now fighting for and representing myself, and Charlie, I remained cool, calm, and collected with a sprinkling of firmness; otherwise he would have torn me apart. But for me, taking everything into consideration, If I'd have lost my rag it would have been fatal for me, not to mention the damage it could have done to Charlie and his progression through the prison system.

Once we had finished filming, Piers shook my hand and said that I argued my point well – I was happy with that. I received no help or preparation for that interview, so I was pleased with the way I conducted myself. Nevertheless, when I watched it back, I could barely pull my hands from my eyes to look. But seeing as it was the first live interview I had ever done, I was content and relatively happy. I was of course nervous the whole way through, not least when I remembered how much bigger TV makes you look, which is true. Apparently the camera adds about 12lb (almost a stone) to your frame.

During this time while representing Charlie to the media I was forever seeking Rod's approval, still nothing I ever did was ever right in Rod's eyes, and not once did he thank me for what I'd done or been through. Once back home, messages from all over the world came flooding in, and certain individuals on social media began their witch hunt towards me; this was something that went beyond what would be considered constructive criticism. Apparently, the whole country was talking about my appearance with Piers, and as informed by a friend, I was number one trending on Google. I got myself home to a safe sanctuary, and locked myself in, but for some reason, suddenly I felt extremely isolated – I just wanted to see Charlie. But unfortunately, that wasn't to be, 'cos my next visit was a whole week away.

A week later, I made my way, V.O (visiting order) in hand to see him. Charlie instantly expressed how happy he was with me, and due to his positive approval, my anxiety melted away. Charlie had a way about him and could always make me feel safe and strong, that was at least until the time came for me to leave. And true to form, from that day to this, while visiting Wakefield nick, certain people would congratulate me, while others would snigger, mock and gossip; it very quickly became the norm.

I got talking to one really nice woman, she came to the wedding reception with her children, I would always love it if we were on visits the same day because she would calm me right down, otherwise I'd be in a panic, trowelling on more makeup in the toilet and perfuming myself to within an inch of my life. I always wanted to look my best which turned into something of an obsession. It was a difficult time with a lot of pressure, plus I was forever fighting against the cruel and uncalled for comments that were written about me in the media. And because of all this, I felt I desperately needed to build up a thick skin; simply aesthetic, but momentarily, somehow it made me feel shielded and protected.

It's official, by now everyone knew that I was Charlie's fiancé. I had hundreds of messages coming in on a daily basis, and the nice supportive ones I made an extra special point of replying to; but obviously in and among these messages came an overabundance of twats, similar to the ones that I'd been receiving for the past year, and these I have to confess really took it out of me. Still hey, who am I to argue with stupid.

Charlie wanted me to attend certain charity events where I would have to auction off art in the boxing ring and, in my heels, put on a right show for the crowds: Charlie knew that on his behalf I would refuse to exit those ropes until enough money had been thrown into the charity-coffers. Charlie loved to listen to me as I would recall the stories of how I worked and helped charities and individuals; most of these people would thank Charlie, personally, I can't say I ever got the merest of mentions. One lady who never forgot me was a lovely woman who lived local to me called, Barbara Dransfield, this lady and her sweet, late husband were extremely supportive to me, and I shall never forget them for that.

One of Charlie's devout followers, who strangely referred to Charlie as 'The Boss" had warned me before I started visiting Charlie that he sees loads of women and that he would always be the same, he said: "He will never get out of prison, and you will be nothing special to him!" However, at that time, me and my delusional mind simply thought, 'Erm, we will see'. Anyway, Charlie wanted me to present Babs with £1000 in cash, so I drove over to Ashton in such a rush, then after jumping from the car in some haste, I fell right down the slippery bank but collected myself and presented the cash to a very shocked and surprised Babs. Charlie also called me while I was with her and I presented her with some artwork, too.

Babs was emotional and broke down in tears, for Charlie had been her beacon of hope ever since she was attacked by some thugs who broke into her home and left her for dead. She showed me pics (that hadn't been released publicly) from hospital, and after seeing them I swear to God I would happily have done a life sentence for murdering those cowardly bastards. Later I said to Charlie that "Unlike you Charlie, I would do the deed, do my time cleverly working the system and be out in about seven or so years." With regard to the Bab's incident, Charlie agreed to do another photo session and interview, but it took me over a month of pursuing and persuading them to cover such a positive Charlie story. As I'm sure you're aware, the media never want uplifting stories on Charlie, most only wanted dark Bronson stories. Stories about how kind hearted he truly was don't usually sell papers. My endeavours to have decent stories printed about Charlie were often fruitless, and a complete waste of my time and efforts.

So, what was my job now? Well as soon as the engagement news broke, within 48 hours I was sacked from every company I worked for, further-more, my agent dumped me after a couple of months, saying: "You will always be Bronson's bird now!" They said that they could no longer put me forward for the sweet young mummy and family roles for commercials etc. They also said that no casting director in the country would employ me. I guess I could see their point! At which point I became chief secretary for the Charlie Bronson empire, which is a whole lot bigger than many would believe. My job entailed, sending out signed photos and dealing with Charlie's art, and any profit made from said revenue would be split equally, unless of course it was for charity, and most were sold and auctioned for charity.

Being Charlies girlfriend and secretary did not come as a paid position, and slowly but surely my savings were depleting. Fortunately, at this time, the ITV show 'Loose Women' wanted to book me, and without a seconds thought, I decided to do it. At the time, I remember being nervous, yet excited. It was a show that I knew reasonably well having watched and enjoyed it many times, so seeing it all backstage was a little surreal. I was very well looked after by the team, but Jane Moore and I clashed a lot, in fact I felt very isolated sat along-side them on the panel, but off screen the girls were all lovely.

For once, Coleen Nolan was very quiet, but in the break, she expressed how sorry she was for not speaking up, and that she genuinely really understood me and liked me. She said that she was at ease sat behind the scenes defending me, but on screen couldn't bring herself to say the things she knew were right. She also said, she could see that I was an honest girl and that she was worried for me. I assured her, as I did to all the women on air. Then it's over and you are quickly ushered out to waiting paparazzi. I didn't expect them at all but I turned to them, glanced a little smile, then promptly got into an awaiting car.

Instead of heading to Euston I went to Soho to meet one of my close friends in our usual Compton's. It's a gay bar and usually full of men and I always sat at the back if it was available, and it was. I needed a drink and to calm down, James (the same James I took to Blind Beggar) had watched the show and told me he thought I'd done really well. We decided to just be our normal selves and not talk about it. We spent most of the day out and then went dancing. Nothing frees me like dancing and downstairs at 'Halfway to Heaven' is where we often head as there is always a good drag act on. I love drag queens, with their sharp tongues' and overtly to-the-point demeanour. I only wish I could show on stage how I handle the role of mental people in person, aided with prosecco and gin.

Chapter Nine: Pap and What The Rats See

One day Colin and I were watching something called 'Confessions of a Paparazzi' and there was this bloke who was so funny but had no morals. The man was a maverick, revealing crazy things about the paparazzi and how they go about their work. This was of interest to me, given the fact that I now had some experience with the 'paps'. I was honestly laughing out loud in parts, mind you, I could see that this fella was essentially a bit of a numpty; he was a cheeky chappy and reminded me a bit of my brother, Andrew. I searched social media and found him on twitter and in the hope of seeing more of his antics I began following him, however, I was very quickly distracted and immediately forgot about him.

About 3 weeks later I got a follow back and he messaged me asking if I was engaged to Charles Bronson, "Yes!" I replied. "The one and only, at your service." And that was that, he was hooked. Thinking about it with hindsight I imagine he could smell a money-making opportunity and that was where his interest started. Soon after our initial "e-meet" he flagged up the notion of working with me. However, because I didn't want to make a mockery of me and Charlie, I very quickly declined all of his offers.

Bamby obviously knew lot of people at the national papers and as bait to my ego quickly threw up a plethora of famous names that he was on speaking terms with names like Gordon Ramsay and David Cameron, saying he was sure he could get them to make a comment in positive support of Charlie and his progression through the prison system.

Now, Bamby is like Charlie and also my dad: an absolute charmer and exceptionally quick-witted and funny to-boot! And before long he began messaging me daily in the hope of getting involved with the work I was doing towards Charlie's cause. I had already started a petition that I hoped to personally hand to the Prime Minister at 10 Downing Street and Bamby said he could muster up lots of interest from the relevant people to back us in our efforts. With that he shared it on social media and the numbers quickly began to rise. Of course, Rod had also been plugging it and with the new flurry of interest, it swiftly became an obsession of mine to get this elevating number up and above 10,000, which was the same amount his former wife Lorraine had reached during her tenure.

The work for me was gruelling and I was often up until 3am sending pertinent Bronson information to various groups. I was also privately chatting with Charlie's ever-growing supporters as I delicately urged them to champion his cause and share the information they were now in possession of. And slowly but surely my entire life became overwhelmingly devoted to Charlie and his campaign.

One morning a friend called me up to inform me that I was once again splashed all over the Daily Mail and Sun online, stating that I was pen-pals with: oh, I cannot even bring myself to utter his name, because, as Lee, my writer friend has just flagged-up, having our names in print next to the murderer's for the rest of eternity fills him with disgust. So, for the purposes of this chapter we shall refer to this sick and evil monster simply as, 'Child-Killer'! At this point I would just like to point out one simple fact that the world and his wife are privy to: This man is a bonafide MONSTER! A heartless, non-human and gutter-dog, void of any respect for life and all its creations. Unlike my Charlie, who never killed a soul and would protect, with his life, children and anyone else for that matter from these contemptible, loathsome, scumbags. Nevertheless, and for the record, many, many years before my engagement to Charlie, I was in touch with said scumbag. However, I was furious and clearly very anxious at the flagging up of this, and the calls, messages and cyber bullying that was roused (which never stopped) came flooding into my inbox. This, of course, was crippling to my mental state and hit me like a full-on Pearl Harbour attack. However, for the brainless idiots who chose to believe that this gutter-dog and I were actually friends, here is the truth…

So, in 2002, I did correspond with said CK (Child-Killer), but purely as part of my research while I was studying for my drama degree at university. What these brainless and boss-eyed cretins weren't privy to was that I used to catch the same bus as Winnie Johnson, who was the mother of the missing boy Keith Bennett, who, I might add, in justification, was aware of my brief correspondence with the scumbag of all scumbags and, having a brain to see what my game was, totally backed me in my endeavour for research purposes.

Lots of people had written to the CK, and some even struck up a friendship with him. Not moi, *oh the very thought!* The man was an out-and-out psychopath, which was abundantly obvious, and once I'd gathered the vaguest of answers to my questions, I immediately ceased my connection. However, he then began answering my earlier questions, such as: "Could you tell me what areas are of interest, to you?" At which point (in the same way he did with everybody up until his death) he started to play cat and mouse with me. And my initial hopes of wedeling out information re Keith Bennett and his whereabouts quickly collapsed. I'll give him one compliment; he was far from stupid and knew exactly what I was drilling for.

A little time after, fortuitously as the news hit that Myra had kicked the bucket (good riddance), I was one of the people on the same bus trying to comfort Winnie. This poor, grief laden lady was distraught, saying: "Well that's that: I will never ever find my Keith, now!" To console her I promised her that I would try. Unfortunately, soon after, I had to cease correspondence with him because it was quite obvious that I, like everybody else who was in contact with him (Winnie too), we were simply treated as pawns in his sinister games.

The other part of my plan was to do a play, in soliloquy format, called, 'And all The Children Cried', where I was to play the lead role of the female collaborator of said Child-Killer and any information I managed to get from him would have been invaluable for my studies.

Now, living in Manchester at that time I was fascinated, although obviously disgusted by their crimes, and wanted to see if I could see anything which would draw someone to a man like him. Moreover, in desperation to find the truth for a destroyed Winnie, I promised her that I saw it as a sense of duty to find out anything I could about her beloved boy. The correspondence was brief and contrary to popular belief no gifts were exchanged either way. Look, I never wanted to visit the devil spawn, but obviously the tabloids and their so called, 'sources' alleged the usual crap.

Charlie had known long before about my brief correspondence, and he for one understood it. Charlie also had money sent to Winnie, and because the lovely Winnie and I were on speaking terms, it was something else we would often discuss. So, to the people that had me down as someone who rubbed shoulders with an utter murdering bastard, do you honestly think a man like Charlie would have anything to do with me if he thought such headlines were anything but a pack of newspaper selling lies? Of course, he wouldn't. I loathe and detest the CK, as much, if not more, than the next person.

Over the years I have been to several of the graves of the victims and laid flowers etc, and here I was getting slated for being in cahoots with him. And obviously I would be hard pushed to explain myself every single time that, although I was researching the scumbag, I also had a hidden agenda, and any correspondence received back from him was met with an amount of hostility.

Strangely enough, Charlie used to write to the CK's female collaborator; he would send her two cigarettes a month in the hope of her meeting her maker, quicker. Charlie (of all people) understood and thought it was kind of me to at least try and get Winnie some closure. These abusers on a bullying echelon of social media would post damningly crude pictures of the CK, with my face superimposed on the female collaborators body alongside him. I had hoped to do a deal with a national paper, telling the truth about the whole debacle, but I do believe the editors would have negatively bent the truth, so I immediately cancelled the contract. Anyway, my friends knew the absolute truth, as do you now.

Chapter Ten: The Gangster's Moll

Sometime before the Weinstein scandal, my agent, who had recently dumped me, contacted me saying that a production company in Manchester, who were working with the Weinstein company in New York, wanted a meet with me to discuss my hopeful involvement in an upcoming project and a meet was immediately arranged. At the meet they told me they were piloting a UK version of 'Mob Wives' and that they wanted me to be part of it.

My first thought was no, because it would look as though I was using Charlie as a media vehicle, but I chatted with Charlie and he expressed his absolute love for the idea; the idea of me being his 'glamorous fiancé' was fantastic news to him, and for that reason alone he was adamant that his future wife should be totally involved. Coincidentally two friends of mine Frances Shea (who I have previously mentioned) and her daughter, Bonnie, had also been contracted to do it. I spoke to Frances and she aired some reservations, but after chatting at length we both decided to do it.

At this point they were only filming a pilot episode, and we decided that if we didn't like the way they portrayed us, as some kind of desperate characters and not the real people we are, then we would call a halt to doing the series. So, I had another meeting with David from the UK production company in Manchester; I took my friend Colin along with me and at the meet David informed me who else he had lined up for the show; two names I had never heard of before, who for all intense and purpose looked like plastic reality stars. Colin watches reality shows and thought that one of the 'Moll Girls' sisters was in the TV show, 'Love Island' or something similar. To be quite truthful, I had no idea who Colin was talking about, but didn't really care as long as we all got on. We did almost a week of filming for the pilot. I took my neighbours Chihuahua, Portia, along with me, which turned out to be a mistake because she was besotted with me and was forever running into my house through the cat flap. While we were filming it was clear to see that Fran was upset with me over the incident regarding the CK, nevertheless, she's an intelligent lady, and although her and Bonnie were initially shocked, after I'd explained my story, they completely understood and backed me all the way.

We met the other two women who were a bit up themselves. The younger one thought she was some kind of superstar, demanding shots of sambuca at 11am and complaining about absolutely everything. Chrissy the older woman (probably the kind of woman Charlie wanted me to turn into) was always in killer stilettos, fake tan, fake boobs a tight black dress with ladled on makeup like Aunt Sally. Oh, and she had a young boyfriend in tow; he was actually lovely! But these pair, especially the young one, were a nightmare, and their vague claim to 'mob fame' was that Chrissy's dad was one of the most famous robbers the country had ever seen. He must have been good, 'cos not a soul among us had ever heard of him. Worse still, Charlie or any of his associates hadn't a clue either. So, I guess he must have robbed banks in the time it took his wife to cook his dinner. Utterly ridiculous!

The narrative of the show didn't sit very well with me. Frances, Bonnie, and I are real people: these two ladies were born into it, and my involvement came from a genuine love for a man who I fought tooth and nail to change a certain stratum of the public's perception of. To be fair, Chrissy wasn't too bad. At the end of filming she said she was just playing a role, but Lauren the younger one was simply ridiculous, a so-called 'Gangster's Moll' who didn't even know who Charlie Bronson was. I think the producers were merely using her to be the bitch of the group; she wanted so much to be a reality star like her sister, but in the process was extremely disrespectful to everyone involved. This girl certainly wasn't all that! You see I am an actress, and will play a part, but not if it was to the detriment of Charlie's reputation.

It was obvious what the production team wanted, and I tried my hardest to be strong and give them what they needed. However, in the end, even after the thousands of pounds they spent on it, it was decided that it would glamourise crime in the UK and whilst that might work in America it would cause many problems with the powers that be in good ol' blighty. To be truthful, in the end it was a bit of a relief because, for obvious reasons, they wanted to use the name, Bronson and not Salvador. But I wasn't marrying Charlie just so I could become a mob wife, I was marrying him to be a devoted wife and aid his plight to one day see him free. By the way Charlie loved that little pooch, Portia, and had a little pic of her in his cell; he really does have a good heart.

Chapter Eleven: Salvador's Personal Assistant

During this time, it's important to remember that mine and Charlie's relationship was full-on. I was still receiving letters on a daily basis, we were having two-hour long phone calls three times a week, not to mention a two hour visit once a week, so all wasn't as it obviously appeared to the masses. Also, Charlie was sending me letters he'd been sent that he wanted me to check out. Then once I'd read them, I'd have to report back with my views on their intentions, veracity, or simply if the said sender could be in some way useful to him and his progression.

Charlie receives about a 1,000 letters a month, and a lot of those would be delegated to me to go through. One certain man who followed Charlie relentlessly was a fella called Tim Price, now this man really did worship Charlie; so much so in fact, he even had his Saab done with : 'Free Charles Salvador' on it. Tim was certainly committed to the cause and drove me to see Charlie and to events (mostly for charities) that I attended on Charlie's behalf. On one occasion, he also helped me do the merchandise at a boxing event; an event where the man running it couldn't run a piss up in a brewery.

I had done some recordings of Charlie's voice for the show, and he had also done some artwork that was to be auctioned off by me for Maureen Flanagan, (long-term friend of the Krays and their mother's hairdresser) and a Macmillan nurse. However, the prat running it never collected the money and couldn't even get it right when he was attempting to put Charlie's voice on. And for that reason, the majority of guests didn't have a clue what was going on. Fortunately, through sheer determination, a few months later I managed to track the buyer down and he paid in full, then one well known BKB (Bare Knuckle Boxing) man took a shine to me and asked if I'd visit him. I told Charlie about it, 'cos that is simply the way I am. Although, I always left out the shit I got over it; I would always want to protect him from anything like that. Then this BKB man wanted me to go away with him for the weekend. One Sunday morning, shortly after, Charlie called me and said to call this bloke and say that Charlie said, he would have his balls shot off with a sawn-off shotgun if he ever bothered me again – and strangely enough, the correspondence came to an end.

Also, a man who doesn't even deserve to be mentioned but is apparently a man who Charlie knew and was helping Charlie author a book, well he too began slagging me off, as did his wife (who I believe left him soon after) in a big way. I asked him privately what is problem (I did this as I didn't want to harm Charlie's profile) but never got a reply. He then started started slagging Charlie off again. So, one morning I called him up and put him in a three-way call with me and Charlie, and Charlie politely quizzed him about who he was and why he was slagging the two of us off. (As it so happens, Charlie had received said "authors" book and had said the man was completely illiterate!) Anyway, this is what comes from people bullshitting. I was always in the middle of this sort of grief and I often had sweet F.A to do with it. During the call the man became worried - you could hear it in his voice, this was a complete turnaround to the man who was forever instigating rows on Facebook. Charlie also asked him to stop using his name and after that he just message privately saying nice things, so I said: "You live in Wakefield yes? Why don't you meet me at Boon's pub on Friday? I will wait until you and your wife can come, and we can sort this all out?" I then said, "Listen, if we meet up you might actually be surprised." Nonetheless, he made excuses for them both and declined … bloody typical.

I don't use any social media to bully or slag people off, even those who have been vile to me. I simply ask them to meet me and never has one of these bullies taken me up and met me. They are all a bunch of cowardly spineless people hiding behind their keyboards, however when I started getting very personal threats of violence I turned to my little black book of 'naughty' contacts, and an associate of the late 'Guv'nor' Lenny McLean started to watch over me. Through my extensive contacts I had the names of 'faces" in almost every city across the UK that I could call upon if ever I felt threatened. But fortunately, no one actually ever came to physically harm me. Nevertheless, on a daily basis the nasty fuckers on the bully-boy Facebook page (a page made up of toe-rags who apparently looked up to the likes of Charlie and The Twins) insisted on cyber-bullying me to a relentless degree, and I was one of the people they reportedly looked up to's Fiancé. Charlie himself said if this would have been the 60s these particular ringleaders would have been buried by their own idols; their actions were utterly shameful.

One visit, a few months after the announcement of the engagement, Charlie said we should call it off. I thought he was joking. "Call it off? Do you know what I have given up for you, what I endure daily?" "Yeah, I love you for it, but should we bother getting married?" I told him in no uncertain terms that if he was going back on his word, he would lose all respect from me, I had got the petition with over 20,000 signatures which was more than double his last one. My house was becoming an office. My friends dubbed it as 'Salvador Central' because of the paperwork everywhere, how could he even think of calling it off? Then he snapped back and said "Yeah, sorry babe. Course it's on." I left feeling worried.

I had also done couple of radio interviews by now and gone on Loose Women again, this time Katie Price was going to be on the show and on a previous show she said she couldn't understand why I didn't just go to a bar to find a man. (not to mention the fact that Charlie had done a drawing stating she'd had more cock's than a farmyard – which, I might add, was splashed all over the bloody tabloids! Did people really believe I just lured him in and gave up others others on the way. I even gave up a woman who in my eyes, was the most perfect woman on the planet; we had been friends and had a huge amount of history between us, but I chose Charlie over her and it really hurt her. Fortunately though, we remained friends and that will never change.

When I met Katie we got on really well, she found the art funny and was genuinely interested in it all, obviously her question of "Have you done more?" had to be answered. "Sadly no, Katie," I said, "but the truth is this… if there were no bars between us, and a sleeping guard… uh um… well my dear, we'll have to have a proper chat later." I was also with Katie's ex Alex Reid the day before, because George Bamby had got me to agree to do this documentary. We were everywhere doing interviews with people, Alex came to the wedding with his partner. I wish I had more time to chat to Katie that day on Loose Women, I hate to see bullying and I had always stuck up for her in the past. I think she had recently had some surgery when I met her as her face looked unnaturally tight and her eyes looked terribly sore. To be honest I think it's awful how people slag her off for the surgeries and the men in her life, it is up to her what she does with her life. I believe she is a wonderful mother and has clearly felt such pressure to retain her good looks and doesn't know when to stop. I have experienced how cruel people can be and its absolutely horrid and horrendous to read. No matter how thick skinned you are it always hurts.

I was on my way to do a radio interview for BBC Radio 5 Live and had an awful cold. I was sat in the back whilst the driver was taking me to the studios and Bamby rang "What is it?" I asked. I was full of cold and trying to do some warmups for my voice because I was worried it would sound terrible on the radio. "Have you ever wondered why I contacted you?" He asked. "Yeh!" I knowingly replied. "So, you could get in on something you believe has a lucrative edge?" To which he replied, "No Paula, there is more…" as he proceeded to tell me more about his past.

I had already caught him out on a couple of things about his past but said nothing, however, I certainly hadn't prepared myself for his next announcement, which was , "Charlie is my dad!" "Fuck off" I said. "He's no more your dad than Father sodding Christmas, I'm full of cold and off to do a radio interview so bugger off". We often spoke to each other in that manner, I told you he reminded me of my brother so I would speak to him with that familiarity, but Bamby would not let it go and kept on and on, "Do you believe me?" "No, I don't!" "But others would and I can prove it." "Then I suggest you prove it, now sod off, I'm not well. And I'm running through things in my head for the interview if this is some kind of stunt please stop it now as this kind of thing could and will cause a lot of damage. Please respect that I introduced you but not for bullshit like this." With that I said goodbye and put the phone down.

Radio 5 DJ Emma Barnett was her usual self and not very warm at all. I managed (while pointing out that he was a nonce) to take the opportunity to mention that John Venables had been given all these different identities and has been recalled to prison so the government should stop wasting money on the likes of him and allow Charlie to progress. I mean, who could argue with those facts? I would do these shows and get terrible anxiety but I did them for love and I utterly believed in my fiancé. There was never any money in radio interviews so if I didn't believe in him I would never of done any media and after every bloody one I faced a torrent of abuse.

Rod and Bamby don't get on and never have, Rod didn't like Bamby from the start but instead of telling him he would ring me to bitch about him or tell me things he would want him to know via me. I often found it strange that things would forever go thru me and at times it was tearing me apart and my anxiety would take over to the point where I was being sick 2-3 times a day or more. Charlie wanted ridiculous things in the press, Rod wanted his own agenda, stuff sending and particular stories, which I endeavoured to do if it helped Charlie. Bamby wanted ludicrous stories and I just would not be a part of those.

After the radio interview that day I got home and wrote Charlie a letter. My tone was that of someone who loved him dearly and I said if Bamby contacts you with any ideas that are false please, please, do not go along with it as it will cause so much trouble - I was very clear. I got a letter back from Charlie telling me not to worry but I was worrying as I knew what this would do.

I now had to get preparations ready for the wedding which was no easy task, Charlie had paid the money his end to the prison authorities and I wanted it to be a religious ceremony but the vicar didn't turn up on a visit when he was supposed to. This pissed Charlie off royally, I explained that there was probably a reasonable explanation but Charlie was having none of it, he didn't want a pie and liquor (vicar) doing the service anyhow. He had only agreed because of me, this made my job worse. I could never get through to the vicar so I had to write to him but got no reply. On my next visit I asked for Father Paul, the vicar, to come and see us in the seg unit but he didn't so this utterly cemented it. Not only would I be marrying in a prison instead of a lovely old church as I had always dreamed of, but there was going to be no religious significance whatsoever. I wrote a shitty letter to Father Paul and this time he called me back and I ended up apologising to him and said again the position I was in. I told him where I worshipped and how important it was but there was no going back now. I could have sorted it but Charlie's mind was made up. There was something else now also playing on my mind.

About a year ago a female friend of Charlie's who has a boyfriend and who claims to be a close friend (I had no reason to disbelieve her until Charlie said what he did) had mentioned in a chat between myself and the man who called Charlie 'The Boss', that once Charlie had said to her they should get married so he can have a party. Charlie had told me previously that she was really just a partner of his friend. If this was true how many other women friends had he said this too? Was it in jest? It was another worrying signal, which I put to the back of my mind as I believe I can tell if a person is truthful or not by their eyes. I don't trust anyone who doesn't make eye contact with me. Charlies eyes were full of sparkle and love. I know he loved me.

I was back and forth to the Registrar in Wakefield Registry Office. What would have been a simple task for any other couple wishing to marry was a mammoth task for us and probably for many others who get married in prison. I was back and forth with calls, emails; not to mention the hours of daily correspondence with supporters and I still had an actual wedding and reception to plan, but first there was another extremely important thing.

Charlie wanted a 10 Downing Street 'March For Justice' organising for his birthday, which is the 6th September. However, obviously due to political red-tape it isn't that easy to arrange. Instead, I could get it booked with Parliament for the 7th, so Rod came up with the idea of doing two marches with petition handovers as well. The first march was on Charlies birthday. He had said that the banner wasn't current enough, so I called Bamby who got one designed and ordered. As my manager I also asked him to get as much media coverage as possible. It took a lot of organising and planning and Rod suggested a different pub to meet in each day which was a big help.

The day before I asked Bamby who he had contacted, and he shouted at me to not ask questions as he didn't have time to report back to me all the time. I never asked him to, but this was important. I called around myself and no one had heard from Bamby and said it was too short notice to do anything now. Clearly as this didn't involve making money he hadn't bothered. I know he had been busy building the true crime museum, but this was the kind of thing I needed him and his contacts for! I called Martin Brunt from Sky News who is a really decent and caring man and he assured me he would try to get there or at least have someone cover it.

There was a small turnout compared to other protests, as Rod was quick to remind me every five minutes. But rather than concentrate on the numbers we didn't have, I chose to concentrate on the numbers we did. I was forever trying to see the positives, even though I am always fighting my own negative demons. The other thing was, I had become a bit of a recluse and, apart from going to the post office to sort and send Charlie's mail and affairs. So, hurling myself to London to lead a protest came purely from the desire to help my husband in any way I could. Some of his supporters thought I was fame hungry, but they should have seen what I did on a daily basis, these people didn't know me, but judged me anyway. As for the media, Rod very clearly said I should handle that side of things (and take the flak from the public along with it!) He said he would do the charity side of things and Daz could run the site. Daz is the man who called Charlie 'The Boss.' Well, he never came to London, I understood that people had other commitments but was disappointed that people couldn't make at least one of the days.

On the day of the MOJ (Ministry of Justice) handover, Bamby and Bev Straker had a big falling out. Bev was outside the Ministry of Justice smoking one of her special cigarettes and Bamby kept referring to Charlie's 'evil past' and both were shouting stuff down a megaphone attracting the wrong type of attention. We finished the day in the pub of course and Tim was doing press ups with me straddled over his back and we were just having a laugh, but Bev went mad and said I was a tart and making a fool of myself. I told Charlie about it and he laughed his head off.

The next day we were heading to Downing Street. Bev was still going on at me, but there was a slightly better turnout this time, so off we went armed with a load of leaflets to hand out to people on the way. "I just want justice for my husband, 44 years behind bars, 38 in solitary confinement, he has never killed anyone or raped anyone, he has raised over half a million pounds for charity, why is he still there?" Anyway, the whole affair was over before it bloody started. I just hoped we'd hit the right notes.

Chapter Twelve: Salvador's Darlin'

Over a period of time Charlie had mentioned that he wanted me there at his next parole hearing, which just happened to be a week to the day before us getting married. I had worked my arse off to get a positive parole dossier together; Rod had helped with certain parts, and while using his knowledge and contacts I contacted charities and individuals that Charlie supported and asked them if they would kindly write a letter documenting such. (Many responded and a handful didn't.) It was a mammoth task and at the end of my work I made copies of all of the documents and added them to my dossier.

In attendance on the day were, three judges, Charlie's solicitor, who I spoke to very regularly, a probation officer and a slightly nervous me. I watched on as Charlie steadily perused through my documents and by the expressions on his face it was clear to see that he couldn't believe the amount of work I had put in. For the hearing I wore a very formal business dress suit, and at first glance I could tell that Charlie hadn't recognised me, I think he thought I was someone from his legal team, but momentarily after adjusting his eye's he realised it was me and gave me a cheeky wink, and I responded back with a sexy wink in acknowledgment.

The proceedings opened, with Charlie speaking first, then his solicitor, and finally me. To be honest, I hadn't really prepared a verbal speech, I simply spoke from heart and head, which got more and more extensive as my confidence escalated; in the end I thought I was playing the lead role in some court room drama. However, all I truly remember was me saying most men of Charlie's age are set in their ways and are incapable of change, but this man I'm going to marry has changed his life entirely and all for the better. I also stated that I was an intelligent lady and certainly would not have married the Charles Bronson of yesteryear but would, without a seconds thought, marry the new and improved Charles Salvador. I looked over at Charlie and he nodded, and I saw his eyes well-up, and immediately so did mine. That emotional nod from him to me was filled with gratitude, love, and respect, and once it was over the solicitor, Charlie and I all got to spend some time together.

Charlie thanked me for the work I had done; I thought there would have been a little more emotion from him, but I guess he'd passed his emotional peak during the hearing. By this time it was lunchtime. Charlie was hungry and wanted to go back to his cell, so we went our separate ways and Charlie's solicitor and I went for a swift gin and tonic in celebration and relief. I got on very well with his solicitor at that time, he devoted so much free time to help Charlie, but unfortunately Charlie dismissed him sometime later. During his time working for Charlie I think he made a mistake, of which he was certainly sorry, but hey, that's Charlie. Once he's made his mind up and he's done with you, he simply erases you from his life - for Charlie, it's as easy as turning off a light.

So, after the parole hearing we barely had any time together. I had managed to fit in another visit, but due to my heavy schedule at that time I was cutting it really fine. I had also (as always) put myself under great pressure to look good and would often change my mind on what outfit to wear, several times, and because of this I left the house in a terrible rush and had my foot to the floor all the way to the prison.

On this occasion, unfortunately, after clearing myself with security and getting Charlie's canteen, I was a rather unacceptable twenty-three minutes late. Anyway, when I finally got to Charlie he was pacing up-and-down like a baying tiger and looked nothing like the man I knew. I immediately tried to excuse my lateness - pleading that it was my fault etc, etc, when suddenly he barked: "Shut the fuck up and sit down!" Never before had I been spoken to in this manner, I was shocked and stunned and instantly (unlike me) did as I was told; if any other person had spoken to me in that way, I would usually give them what for, and that would be that. However, this time was different, this order was given by a man known to the media as Charlie Bronson the scariest inmate in the system.

Immediately, the prison officer tried to reason with him, and again I stood up and said, "Look, don't blame him, it's my fault, and I will tell you why!" At which point Charlie snapped, aggressively and said: "Don't fuckin' bother, and listen, nobody is late for my visits, no one told me nuffin'! If you are late, call the prison and cancel the V.O. I won't accept this from you or anyone!" I tried to tell him that sometimes unforeseen things happen, like traffic etc. But he was having none of it and said: "I don't care, end of fuckin' discussion!" I will admit, his eyes frightened me, it's not often I feel fear, but I was glad of those bars between us that day. Anyway, with that and like the turning on of a tap, he switched back to the person I knew. For me, that was something of a turning point, because that was a Charlie I really didn't think I'd ever be witness to. Food for thought, I guess.

After arriving home that evening, and for most of that night I was on edge. So, to help calm me down I went to a local pub, ordered a brandy, and sat pondering on the day's events. Now, this must have hit me hard, because even at that time I was still shaking a little. I called Bamby who was on holiday, he kind of became my confidante; I know he was paparazzi and a bit of a maverick, but he was actually very comforting to me and said: "Look Paula, I care about you, fuck it all off if you are scared or having doubts, don't go through with any of it!" I thanked him for his support and told him that I was OK (which was a lie), but just needed to talk to a friend.

Talking about friends, Tim Crowley was another who I checked out and introduced to Charlie, and the reason I arranged a meet for Tim was that he had asked me if he could be Charlie's look alike. Charlie and I discussed it and I arranged a couple of visits prior to a photoshoot at Littledean Prison in Glouces-ter (always reminds me of Fred and Rose West) where we did a shoot with my friend in the photographer's seat. Tim was really good in the role as Charlie.

Mind you, what helped was that I immediately warmed to him, which was fortunate because I had told him that if I didn't, he would have been thrown into the rubbish skip along with so many others.

Tim became a prominent part on my journey, but sadly never showed me any compassion or support after the announcement of my split from Charlie. To be brutally frank, at first Charlie said Tim looked like a parrot and looked fuck all like him, and having been the only person to have ever of graced the same ten foot of space with them, not to mentioned, twiddled both their 'tashes, I can honestly say that their moustaches are the only thing they have in common; that and the fact that Tim always dressed really smart for a visit. Introductions were something that I became good at, and for Tim Price, George Bamby, and the rest, if not for my intervention, none of them would have got anywhere near Charlie, which was conveniently forgotten once things for my husband and I turned sour. Nevertheless, despite their views and indeed what the gutter-press likes to print, Charlie and I have never broken contact.

One day I came out of church and was hit with the headline which claimed that Tom Hardy or Danny Dyer would father my child! Well for starters, I'd never even heard of Tom Bloody Hardy, and Danny Dyer and I had already danced that dance … Joke … Pissing hell, it wouldn't take long for that little marriage destroyer to circulate, now would it. Charlie and I had discussed children, but this tabloid came as news to me, and as a result of this I was back on GMB with Richard Madeley arguing the toss. During the interview, Richard, made a mistake in regard to one of Charlie's offences, and as the gigantic faux pax aired a threat of libel ensued. My dad was as happy as Larry with that news as he always said that Madeley was a cocky bastard. However, my mum was simply mortified.

With the wedding drawing ever closer, I felt it was time to seek out a venue. So, after some deliberating, I decided to use the Black Horse pub. Strangely enough, after telling the landlord who the do was for, the pricing list elevated considerably. So Bamby sorted a fee out with the York House Hotel, and also printed the invites for us. I was glad of his help, because without him I was on my own. I liked The York House; it had become a familiar place because most nights after a visit I would end up staying there. It was a family run hotel; they all knew me, and I got on great with the whole family. Mind you, during my last stay there, some man tried it on with me. Anyway, Bamby stepped up to the plate and sorted it – he was good like that. At this point I must say this, people can say what they want about him, but he was the only one to help me with the organisation as we got closer to the wedding. My other friend, Colin, though, helped in many other ways. During that time, I have to say, I was totally reliant on the pair of them.

In 2018, I did a programme that featured on Netflix called, The Dark Tourist, which also featured a friend of Charlie's from New Zealand called Andy Jones: Andy was a lovely family man. I received no money for this piece of film.

As with most things I ever did for Charlie, I did them all for gratis; I did them all simply to help Charlie.

At this point in time I was very ill, but I fought through it and even did a video for the popular 'Vice' channel which, I might add, I never received a single penny. And again, all to help Charlie. Every time I did anything that gained media attention, the despicable Facebook group would mock me and were utterly cruel in their approach and the comments in support of this disgusting debacle were like fuel to an already rising flame. Oh, and if people (not just my friends) stuck up for me, they were ridiculed, laughed at, and promptly barred from the group.

At this time, a great many people began contacting me expressing their utter disgust at this particular Facebook group and its treatment of me. Furthermore, they added that the site should be taken down by the hierarchy at Facebook. Each and everyday my pity towards these nonsensical bullies grew, but the messages of support for me and my one woman battle with these gutter-dogs spurred me on immensely. But still the bullies came! It was getting intense! Apparently, the site and its owners were often asked why they were so obsessed with me and my lifestyle, but questions of this ilk always seem to fall on deaf ears …I wonder why?

This all started a while back by a man that years earlier suggested we do a Christmas collection for Charlie, who (God only knows why) was now claiming that I had not sent the money in, or worse still had pocketed the majority of it. This was a man who used false names, false pictures of himself and mocked the murders that the Cromwell Street lunatics carried out; this individual is a disgusting waste of a human carcass; a carcass that could have been the housing for a soul of peace and purpose. I quickly found out his true identity, these idiots thought I knew nothing … how wrong they bloody were. I immediately told Charlie, that at this particular stage in my life I could quite happily have done time for what I had planned for them, but Charlie (a person people tag as an animal) talked me out of it. So, to these bullies 'of the highest order' I say this: you were extremely lucky that day because Charlie's intervention was your saviour.

Also, around this time I was contacted by Anthony Thomas and his pal who had written a few book's about Lenny Mclean and had just started a new interviewing project called Gangland Podcasts. The two of them also ran social media platforms and had noticed the way I was getting bullied by these cyber trolls and asked me onto their podcast show to set the record straight. The interview was over 2 hour's long and it ignited a sibling like friendship with the other one, Lee. And from that day to this, Lee, my co-author, has supported me through thick and thin.

Now, with the big day looming I very quickly realised I had literally tons of preparation to do. So to start the ball rolling I phoned a friend of mine, Bev

Straker, and asked her if she would take care of the security. Now, for the purposes of this chapter, Bev, is a tough East End lesbian, a bit of a nutter with a souped-up mobility scooter and a bag o' pills for order. She would often accompany one of Britain's first ever page three girls, Maureen Flanagan, to her many engagements and events; all of which will become relevant as you read on. Bev also did security for 'The Yellow Pages of British Crime', Dave Courtney.

While on the subject of Flanagan, I would first like to say that my trust in her waned somewhat after she set me up at Dave Courtney's house, when she told me that Dave had invited me to stop there at one of his parties, which wasn't true, not to mention the fact that my ex was in attendance. This of course was a shock to me, and Flan knew it. Anyway, Flan had been on the phone pleading with me to go along to Dave's, but at the time I was at Toby's house. He'd had a few too many and I wanted to stay with him, but that wasn't to be as Flan went on and on at me until I finally cracked and ordered a cab to take me to Dave Courtney's house, known among the criminal fraternity as Camelot Castle.

On the journey over I was that anxious I had to ask the cabby (driver) to stop while I threw up. When we eventually arrived, it was clear to see that my arrival was unexpected, and Maureen Flanagan, who coaxed me to come along hardly spoke a word to me. I slept on the sofa because all the rooms there were occupied; I felt vulnerable and alone, but fortunately two men stood guard and watched over me. The next day the gossip starting quickly spreading, stating that I had entered into some lude acts with these men etc. However, and sorry if this sounds a little crass, but I was on my period and my tampon was completely intact. Moreover, even after a night of heavy drinking I think I'd have been aware of any sexual activity because, as many will tell you, I can drink any man under the table. Nevertheless, I do remember a sudden feeling of exhaustion that came over me, quite prominent too, almost to the point of collapse. And to this day, I truly believe my drink had been tampered with.

Later that day I learned that Michael Coleman had been cruelly pulled into this game and that Flanagan had convinced me to come then gossiped about me once I arrived; apparently saying 'what a cheek I'd had to turn up uninvited.' And for that reason alone, I have never trusted the woman since. Anyway, I went back to Toby's house, and, bless him, he looked after me as he always did. I learned a lot that night about people and the trust I had afforded them – never again!

Chapter Thirteen: The Final Countdown

I woke up the day before the wedding on November 16th, 2017 in my house. I was remarkably calm with just a hint of butterflies. The past few months had been nonstop work as I was organising the wedding and to add to the mayhem, recently a fresh couple of problems had reared their ugly heads. Charlie had rung me in a rage the day before stating that the Governor had stopped two of our five guests from attending our ceremony, these were, George Bamby and Shaun 'Basky' Baskerville who had both received official letters stating that they would not be allowed into the prison for the ceremony.

I was disappointed; although unsurprised. The upshot of it was that Bamby on our last visit had bragged to the Prison Officer escorting us that he worked as a paparazzi photographer and boasted of his earnings: £10k for a single picture! And as he overly boasted, I stood cringing in the knowledge that such a comment could have disastrous effects. As for Shaun, 'Basky' Baskerville, I personally knew that his house had recently been raided for lethal weapons which he keeps in a locked-up gun cabinet; he'd never used them but was busted for possession.

As it was, Basky and I grew up in the same area and I knew he was a decent bloke, but someone had grassed him up to the powers that be and consequently he had been taken off the list. Apparently Charlie immediately met this decision with fury and demanded they got it sorted – but the only thing I could do was to ask the No.1, that being the Governor Mr David Harding or the Seg Governor Mr Mark Doherty to come to us on our visit, and this was planned for today, the eve of my wedding.

I was sorry they couldn't come but I understood their reasons, although Charlie being Charlie, didn't. Also, another bombshell they dropped was the fact that we wouldn't be allowed our wedding photographs; photographs that Charlie had already paid for himself. He wasn't happy. In addition, we had legally signed a contract which said we could have 22 photos on the proviso they wouldn't be publicised. This devastated me but I was determined to fight it. Media attention had backfired on us, so in Charlie's mind he felt we'd been completely 'mugged off' yet again and he was furious. However, I had other things to sort out, but hoped to chat and reason with one of the Governors on my next visit to the prison.

As is me, I had chosen my dress right at last moment, which fortunately needed no alterations. I had another dress kindly sent to me that I had made smaller but somehow knew it wasn't the one. Colin and I went to the wedding shop where I tried some others and then said to the assistant: "Show me the most beautiful dress you have?" At which point and from out of nowhere, they produced the dress fit for a Princess. 'This is the one', I thought, and promptly paid for it myself.

Charlie had arranged the transfer of £3000 to cover the wedding arrangements. I was trying to cover the cost myself, but he insisted on paying

Paula: As seen through the imagination of (Artist) Carlota Diaz Fernandez
Instagram: (shevintageart)
Celestial Soul: Pounced on by negativity - flounced by mental instability.

Tranquility in Rock-Flower with my loyal friend Teddy.

The names Williamson... Paula Williamson... shaking until stirred.

Left: Sharing a glass or two of liquid-serenity w my beautiful nephew Darren Knapper and my mum.

Life was forever sweet with my
feline boy, Leo.

With my dad Clive, paying homage
to the fallen on D-Day.

With lifelong friend and fellow
comedienne Claire Jones. For
a time we were the 'Girls on Top'.

Forever friends: From L-R: Star, Kimmy, Bev,
Moi, Jules, Claire and Caz - with Jade
(Star's daughter) watching my back.

My hope was to 'Rock' this dress as
much as the 'School' rocked
the stage.

'I do thee Wed'

My most favourite photograph ever:
pictured at home with my adopted niece.
Life was always joyful when she was around.

Talk about life behind a veil. Here
I am pictured in 'cloak-and-dagger'
mode about to become Mrs Salvad

So happy to have the support of my family.
Taken on my Wedding day with my handsome
nephew's and my brother, Andrew.

On the campaign
trail.

Morgan tried his best to rattle me ...
but this girl just wasn't for rattling.

No Richard my name is Paula!
Anyway... who on earth is Me'Julie?

Hitting the freedom campaign hard
with my dear friend Neil Highlander.

At time's life gets in the way of love.
Pictured with my mum, Hazel.

Behind the scenes of Loose Women
th Kelly Osbourne ...a girl after my own heart.

A relationship - a wedding - and the 'catalyst' that saw the whole thing implode.

Oops sorry Charlie ... you don't want
a divorce for the slight button
malfunction do ya'?

A Freudian slip beneath The Sun.

The annulment was imminent!

Those Trolls' never let me be.

The 'Buoy' I clung to.
However, he was all man,
and a gentle man at that.

for it, and thank god for that. Although, it didn't cover everything, and yet again my savings took a bit of a hammering.

It took us about two hours to get to Wakefield including the stops, because Bamby said he was ill, got out of the car, said he was having a heart attack then swiftly recovered?! Once in the hotel (a place I'd stopped many nights before) the staff were as lovely as ever, but I had no time to hang around chatting. Being late for Charlie was simply not an option (remember me telling you about the incident when I was 23.5 minutes late?!) I got to the Visitors Reception Room with Bamby as usual and spotted no 'paps' - which calmed me somewhat. I begged them to send one of the Governors to come and see Charlie and I on the visit, they radioed through and Prison Seg Governor: Mark Docherty said he would come down and I thanked them (and him) profusely.

The only problem I had was that Bamby was due to come on this visit too but once we set foot in the place he was promptly informed that he was banned, he was actually quite upset but I told him to have a rest at the hotel and that I'd let him know when I was out and then he could come and pick me up; to protect me once again from the swarms of over-eager 'paps'. Bamby takes his camera everywhere and siezed the opportunity of taking some pics of me right before the visit and a quick interview for the documentary. In the brief interview, I simply said I was looking forward to seeing Charlie, but secretly I was worried to death what he'd be like because of the bad news we'd received from the powers that be.

So, I went through all the usual security checks and was on my way. I chose to wear a black chiffon blouse, skinny blue jeans, and long black thigh high boots with a beige coat. I got to Charlie's canteen and spent around £17 on his usual favourites which always consisted of: pork pies, pastries, sandwiches; fruit; sweets; mints; chocolate and tea – with no hot water, (teabag in a cup) Charlie always has his flask of hot water and makes his own tea (fussy bugger). It's always something of a ceremony when Charlie makes his 'Rosy Lee' – I jokingly compared it to having high tea with his Landlady Lizzie, you probably know her as, 'Her Royal Highness!'

Charlie immediately wanted to know where Bamby was. I told him that he was stopped by the guards but sends his best wishes. Charlie went on for a while about Bamby not being on the visit, which I found odd, but at least I was bloody there! Charlie likes to see what I'm wearing in full, as he can't see from where he's sat behind the bars, so I move all the chairs and do a little twirl; smooth my hands up and down the contours of my body a la, the 'blonde-bombshell' Marilyn Monroe, and give him a cheeky little wink, and he'd always say: "Gorgeous Paula, you've got a beautiful hourglass figure swee'art!" I'd actually lost a bit of weight, unfortunately it wasn't lost intentionally with will-power and determination, I just kept being sick with bloody nerves. I was also sick on this visit in the not so glam seg (segregation) visitors' toilets. As usual, Charlie passed me a thick wad of letters that he needed me to smuggle out, I immediately hid them down my boots, as they never checked me on my way out, which was ridiculous really. I could've been smuggling anything.

There was a letter for me and a big one for Charlie's best man and best friend, Rod. I never read anyone else's personal letters, so I obviously had no idea what was in his, but I was dying to read mine as usual. The visit was tense, Charlie wasn't happy about losing two of our guests, but I told him I'd do my best at getting them replaced, I also said that at least the photos would be taken (by a screw), so as long as we had them, we'd get them and told him not to bloody worry. With our faces pressed hard against the bars as usual, and after I'd had a mint, we kissed, well no one likes to kiss a person who has recently thrown up! Anyway, I told him to relax and to remember that tomorrow was going to be the start of our lives together.

I reminded him of the pact we had made when I accepted his proposal; I would do everything on the outside to get him progressed through the prison system, and in turn he would do everything on the inside as well; Charlie had agreed to stay calm and not allow himself to get riled up, and the best way to do this was to focus on his art, fitness, and helping the many charities he supports. Oh, and of course, little old me; however, I'm sure that last teasing kiss had given him all the focus he needed! Charlie just had to keep his bloody head down, and I'd sort everything else with Rod and John, Charlie's solicitor in civvy-street. If only Charlie truly knew what I'd been dealing with on the outside; I only told him bits because it upsets him, the fact that there was nothing he could do directly. I mean, of course he knew that Lenny McLean's enforcer friend was keeping an eye on me, which, as you can imagine reassured him no end - and we left it at that. Plus, if you tell Charlie something he doesn't want to hear, he simply closes it down and moves onto another subject, at which point there would only be me who could get through to him about certain things. I may have kept things from him for his own good, but I never lied to him and I always pulled him up if he was in the wrong.

I later discovered that only two of our mutual friends (who had never met Charlie) would tell him if he was in the wrong, and for the record they were, Julie Preston and Beverleigh Zacher; two very abrupt and direct ladies who take no prisoners – oops, pardon the pun. Each time he was told something he didn't like he'd throw his toys out of the pram and send vile letters, but Jules, Bev and I were always there for one another, and never took any of his crap. These two ladies also stuck up for me when Charlie turned on me about my weight gain; something that the tabloids lapped up and went to town on, paralleled in fine bullying style by a plethora of internet trolls – you know who you are.

The visit was passing by quickly, and there was no sign of the Governor, so the Officer guarding got on his radio to track him down. The Officer guarding would, if they weren't being discrete already, be barked at by Charlie to, "Read the fackin' paper and get your head down! Can't ya' see I'm spending some time with me Missus!" And as you would imagine, they did as they were told! As this was a special day, Charlie got a special treat…I'll leave you to create your own image as to what, 'the treat' was! On Loose Women when Katie Price asked me if we'd 'done more?' my answer was, and at that time had to be, "Sadly no!" However, of course we bloody had! We were a right pair! As I'm sure you're finding out as you read this!

So, this visit had afforded Charlie a little 'oral-treat' and he went back to his cell with crimson smudged lip marks as evidence. Charlie loved that part the most, the evidential red lipstick smudge. I suppose for a second or two it made him feel free. For the machismo-fuelled cynical males, my husband has a lovely 'old-boy' with good girth! It's just a pity I never had the chance to fully enjoy it! With our marriage annulment in process he rang me two days ago and said he'd had a few 'ham shanks' over some photos of me and the memories they conjured up; "I went off like a yogurt pot!" he proudly proclaimed before saying "Ay, do you think we will really get to do it one day?" To which I replied in full-on-politician style, "Well, do you, Charlie?" "O'course I fackin' do!" He adamantly demanded! "We'll see Charlie boy! We'll see!" I teased, as I tantrically fondled his desires, (my, my, I lost myself for a moment … sorry to digress … erm anyway, back to our visit!

Charlie was a whole lot calmer after his 'treat' and he leaned in and said he had to tell me something. Now, I haven't told anyone this; I've kept it to myself, but it's been one hell of a thing to keep and it will explain my extended nerves for the following day, in the light of a full-on media frenzy. Charlie leaned towards me and using his gruff yet hushed tone as I listened hard; when he did this it usually meant he needed something sorting on the outside, or sometimes something with the media, but this wasn't a message. I wouldn't even call it a warning; It was a demand for my very own safety.

"Babe, we've been mugged off enough by them now and no one does that to me or my woman. If that prat Harding comes into the room tomorrow, I'm gonna give you a signal, when I do, pick your dress up and run for the fackin' door, because I don't want you to have to witness it: I want you fackin' safe". My heart missed a beat as I pleaded with him: "Charlie, please, please, please don't do anything to upset our wedding; this is my big day! I've dreamt of it ever since I was a little girl. Obviously, it wasn't in a bloody prison. Nevertheless, I love you and I'll marry you anywhere, but please don't do anything stupid?" "No. I've made up my mind, and that's it. I've even shook that twat's hand for you and now he's done this to us? Nobody messes with us like this … look Docherty ain't even here and it's almost time. It's been lie after lie and enough is enough, so just remember the signal babe, okay?"

What could I say? When Charlie makes his mind up that's it. There is literally no stopping him, so if the Governor came into the wedding the next day (which was highly likely) it was gonna kick off in true hardcore 'Bronson Style.' I agree, we had been messed about, something chronic and maybe just maybe they were goading Charlie to get a reaction, as he has (as is well documented) fell out with them enough times. Charlie's mantra: Play fair with Charlie, and in-turn he will play fair with you. These two Governor's certainly hadn't. Was it personal, or were they simply carrying out orders from the hierarchy? (well, we'll get to that later in the book).

Still, I couldn't believe that after everything I'd done, everything I'd given up, and he was going to do whatever it was he'd planned, and on our bloody wedding day as well. Can you imagine the fear inside me? Can you imagine the horror of coming out to a shit load of media; terrified and shaking; blood drenched and dishevelled, like a scene from that movie, 'Carrie'. Not to mention the fact that I wouldn't be able to sodding run fast in the dress I'd chosen, it was huge - and utterly beautiful; it was what I'd dreamed of and Charlie was the man I believed in, and ultimately wanted a life with and he'd just said that!
Then before we knew it, he was back to his cheery self, getting ready to be taken back for his tea (that's dinner to you southern lot) "Bye Babe, aye, I can't wait to see you tomorrow, this is it! Us against the world! Love ya!" And with that the guards' cuffed him, and he was gone.

I had to go to the toilet for a few minutes just to get my head together, I had Bamby and those lot waiting, and a lot of guests were staying for two nights like us and would be arriving at The York House Hotel by now and I had to face them after hearing what Charlie was threatening. I sunk my head into my hands and prayed that his threats would just fade for another day. A single tear fell from my eye but was quickly wiped away. I was ready to go…

I walked with 'the herd' to get out of the visiting quarters as a quartet of whispering, glaring women bore their eyes into my back. I'd managed to get a few congratulations over the past few months, but I could tell a lot of the women thought I was up my own arse. However, kids are always drawn to me and as I chatted to the 'witches coven's' little-ones, heart breaking as it was to see them tearful as they visited their daddies in prison, I managed to play little games with them, with the hope of allaying their sadness, even if for just a few moments.
A lot of the women warmed to me and asked questions; questions they had probably been dying to ask me, and me being me I'd always oblige and end up having a good old conversation with them. Then, out of the corner of my eye I spotted the Segregation Governor Mr Mark Doherty.

Now, I don't know who I thought I was, but I ran across to him and startled him by abruptly grabbing him by the arm, then I simply smiled cheekily and said: "Oi, where did you bloody get to? We need to sort out the guests for the wedding tomorrow?" I'd obviously caught him off guard as he stuttered "Erm, erm, yes I was getting to that, but something came up, hope you have a wonderful day." "Hang on" I said. "We've got to sort the guests out, I've only got 3, and my dress is bigger than those three put together!" I explained, in a pleading effort to lighten the mood and get him to help us. He made a call and said that Leighton Frayne could come along as a guest. Leighton was not in the best of health and had said that he was going to struggle coming from Wales and to top it off, Lorraine: Charlie's ex was writing his biography! "Can we have either Tim Crowley (better known as Bronson's lookalike) and Tim Price?" as they were both passed to visit and were also driving the wedding cars.

Docherty made another call. And came back saying that Tim Crowley had a small record so he was out, but said we could have this Price man and Leighton Frayne. Now, let me tell you, Charlie knows Leighton from being inside, who I know is a lovely bloke because I had done a charity auction in Wales with him not too long ago. But anyway, I politely said, "Hang on Gov, (I had clearly taken on the Charlie's lingo!) you're not going to tell me that Leighton, who has a record longer than this room can come but Tim Crowley, who has clearly only got one minor offence, cannot?" It was ludicrous, I mean this man had even served time with Charlie in Broadmoor. "Well, you can take it or leave it Paula!" he said. Still, I pleaded with him, mulishly: "But it makes no sense at all, this is my bloody wedding and we've already been dealt a huge blow over the photos, so please try your best and arrange it for us to have the two Tim's... PLEASE?" I pleaded. "Right, I'm too busy for this! Look, take Frayne or that Price man and I'll sort it - otherwise you'll just have the original three!" "Okay then, please put Tim Price on?" I said, pleasantly. With that he made a quick call and that was that.

I was now allowed to have four guests. I agreeably shook his hand, smiled, and thanked him gratifyingly. To be honest, I really wanted a full-on blazing row with the cocky bastard, but at this point I was at his mercy. I always give a hug or shake hands to seal something. I was attempting to be grateful, even though I knew he had the power to do more but it was so rushed and I was just happy that I got Tim added to the guests list. Nevertheless, I felt bad for the other Tim 'cos I got on well with them both, and so did Charlie. In fact, it was me they first sort of contacted, Crowley to me - Pricey to Charlie who sent me a letter to check him out, which I'd been doing for a few months, but I got them both in to visit. The harsh reality being that both of their letters would've been tossed into the over-flowing bin if I hadn't intervened. They were both extremely eccentric, funny men and Charlie and I got on well with them. Only one could come though, still four is better than three but I'd have loved Tim Crowley to have be granted approval too.

I got out of the prison dying to read my letter, but I felt very low. I rang Bamby as I got out and as arranged several cars were parked up in wait, with the windows down slightly, this was an indication to me that they were indeed 'paps' (I know the tell-tale signs). I walked as quickly as I could to the visitors centre with other visitors, mostly women, to get my belongings. There was no answer from Bamby for a while and I needed him to come and pick me up so I could start greeting guests at the hotel and I still hadn't read my letter. I kept ringing and bloody ringing and eventually he answered, apparently he'd fallen asleep, which I guesswas understandable seeing as he'd driven up from Devon the day before. Having said that, knowing how important it was he could've put his alarm on. Anyway, he came and picked me up and in we went to the hotel, me wearing a huge false smile, although that did change as soon as I saw my friends who had made it up from London and elsewhere. Beverleigh Straker was the first I saw, she was sat by the bar window sipping a vodka and coke, "Alright darlin!" She beamed in her broad cockney accent, "Bloody hell Bev, it's great to see you … glad to see you got here okay?" "Course babe," she said, "Told you I'd be here for you!" I'd asked Bev to do security for the event because someone else had let us down. I offered to pay, of course, and she happily agreed.

I also saw Colin which felt reassuring. Bamby was back to his usual self, "Hello, you must be the famous Beverly Straker?" he enquired in his broad Manchester accent and immediately offered himself up for an endearing hug. Unfortunately, his actions weren't met with the same friendly enthusiasm, her response was a little more straight-up and to the point. "Oi Bamby, that's you is it? Listen, I don't like being spoken to how you speak to women, I'm a fackin' lady and when you was on the phone to me that time you called me babe. Listen, I ain't your fackin' babe… I'm here for my best mate Paula, not for you, OK?" I tried to intercept and bring her round, as did Bamby, who to be honest was very polite. But with that, off she went outside to enjoy one of her many daily spliffs. Anything to bloody calm her down, I thought!

Then I saw Rod and his wife Linda at the bar drinking coffee, I'd only ever met Rod at a party for Charlie's birthday the previous year (despite now speaking to him daily). I never got a smile from him then and I barely got one this time nor his wife Linda either, which surprised me. Anyway, I told them that Charlie was okay. I said he was obviously riled, but I'd managed to calm him down and he was really looking forward to the big day. I told him about the guest situation re Tim Crowley, he didn't seem too bothered though as he didn't have a lot of time for Tim, but Charlie and I did so that was all that mattered. Tim could be a bit of a clown and he wasn't savvy when it came to prison culture, but his heart was in the right place and he really wanted the best for us both. I met a few more guests and then went up to the bridal suite which I was sharing with my then friend Colin. I laid myself on the bed, exhausted, I tried to wash away the things that Charlie had said but I couldn't get them out of my head. I locked myself in the toilet and told Colin I was having pre wedding nerves! I took the letter from my boot and put the other one back in that was intended for Rod and read it to myself:

"Babe, I don't expect you to fully understand, but this is my life and it's now your life and my mum's life they are messing with as she deserves to see the photos. I want you to know that I do love you. I want a life with you. I want it all, but I will not be taken for a mug. if I let them get away with this, what next? I know what will happen to me if it kicks off. I can handle it. I can do it standing on my head but whatever happens just enjoy the reception. you'll then be legally Mrs

*Salvador, be proud. have a dance, a laugh and don't forget about the old lady
thing and the sing song at midnight. I'll hear ya if there's enough of you and
thinking of you walking in to marry me then being the old lady is fucking nuts.
it's brilliant, it's who we are, and I'll never change, nor will you, we'll always win,
and we'll always have a laugh!!
can't wait to see you tomorrow,
love Charlie x"*

The letter made me cry and throw up and I had a panic attack while sitting on the toilet seat. I was so mixed up inside emotionally - it was insane. Here
he was saying he wanted a future with me but that he would ruin our wedding
day if the Governor dared to show his face. This act would effectively put years
onto his sentence and prove all the doubters right in all of their assumptions!
The fact was I did understand, given the fact that this had been his reality for
some 40 odd years. I kissed the letter, washed my hands, brushed my teeth, put
the letter in my bag and went back to my room. The 'Old Lady' reference was
regarding something Charlie and I had secretly conjured up.

Almost immediately Bamby ran into the room with all the crew, this was
the last thing I needed, lots of people in and out of my room as I was trying to
sort other stuff like flowers for Charlies close friends to wear. I confided in Colin
and the make-up lady how terrified I was. Bamby had insisted he be the photographer and no one else was allowed to take photos, which was also printed
on the invitations. The deal we had with the Mirror newspaper worried me, but
Bamby said it was okay because this way we would only get decent shots and
he could send awful ones along to the paper for them to use; of course, these
photo's would then remain his sole property, his copyright, so there he was
taking pictures willy-nilly and also forcefully directing the documentary and overseeing everything.

I love dressing up and turning myself into different characters. And one
sunny day a group of my friends and I went out to a National Trust place, I did
all their makeup and costumes and gave them character names and we stayed
in our chosen characters all day. Well, especially me and my best mate Stoat.
Later, I sent the pics to Charlie and he loved them saying that Edith (which was
me) was a right fit ol' bird! After seeing these photo's Charlie wondered whether
or not I could fool the 'paps' by dressing as Edith again, and, while singing his
favourite song (What a Wonderful World by Louis Armstrong) venture out with
the others (whoever was left) at midnight. Therefore, in preparation I had Bamby
print out some song sheets for the rest of 'em. But midnight tomorrow seemed a
million miles away.

First I had an interview to do with The Mirror but then Bamby wanted
to take some other shots and send them to The Sun. This worried me as I didn't
want to break the deal I had with the Mirror. The lady interviewing me had her
dictaphone and was recording everything. Suddenly, her phone rang, and she

had to go out to take the call, I quickly checked, and her dictaphone had been left on. Bamby was then saying hurry the fuck up so we could sort some 'pap' shots by him and get them in to The Sun as he had a mate there waiting so it was already arranged, I was shouted at to stop waffling in the interview! I told him I'd say what I needed to and then I'd come with him even though lots of guests were now arriving and I wanted to thank them and perhaps all have a meal in the hotel restaurant. I footed the bill, which was the least I could do after people had travelled so far and I felt truly humbled.

Shortly after, the lady came back into the room, I knew what Bamby had said would be picked up, and so asked her to delete it and start afresh; she was reluctant, plus Bamby said "For fuck's sake just carry on, we haven't got time!" I was then stronger and demanded that it was deleted as it was unethical to leave it recording private conversations, but Bamby shouted again and I was too tired to argue and let it roll. However, I knew it would come back to bite me on the arse – which it did.

Bamby had appointed himself my manager and personal photographer; he's a very pushy individual when he wants to be. In addition, he was taking 50% of any money made so no wonder he was pushing me and pushing me. Now, I'm a strong girl but I can only take so much. I make no secret of the fact that I suffer from borderline personality disorder (more of that later), manic depression and extreme anxiety, but as soon as the very rushed interview came to an end I was again whisked away into the car to do some set up shots at a hotel nearby. The shots were done but I really didn't feel right about it and strangely enough nor did Bamby, so I was relieved when we discussed it and chose to scrap the idea.

My guess is that he didn't want to risk losing the money from the Daily Mirror either. Now, don't forget I was utterly relying on that money; some money had come to me all cloak and dagger from the 'Charlie Empire' for the wedding but it was still only enough to do things on a shoestring. I found Rod once we got back to the hotel (he was in his room with Linda) I reached in my boot for his letter from Charlie when Rod asked me if the two cars outside were going to drive us around the block in the morning to the Visitor's Centre and then to the prison. I told him yes, that both the Tim's had kindly offered their services for free and besides Price's matte black Saab had 'Free Charlie Salvador' emblazoned across it, which I thought was very apt and Tim Crowley had had his sky blue old style Mercedes, all washed with a bow on it and 'Just Married' on the back which I thought looked lovely. Rod wasn't happy and said that he would rather walk to the venue than get in either car as he'd be embarrassed to be seen in them.

I thought it was a bloody ungrateful thing to say; if he was so bothered why didn't he help me sort the cars? I'd really had enough for one day so said if he preferred to walk then that was up to him and passed him his note. By now I was looking very tired, some of my closer friends told me to go and rest but I couldn't. Rod never asked how I was when he could clearly see I was exhausted or took me up on the offer of a meal, he simply told me that him and Linda had already eaten elsewhere and were getting an early night and shut the door. I felt that Rod was the only person that I could possibly speak to about what Charlie had earlier said but the chance had gone. I truly was alone.

Colin was now back in the room, so I told him how exhausted I was and we decided to order a bottle of wine up to the room and chill for a while before having to go back downstairs. However, no sooner had the wine arrived then so did Bamby and his crew and Tim Crowley (Charlie lookalike). Apparently they wanted to do a dance sequence hash-up that looked like I was having a smooch with Charlie. I agreed, reluctantly, but only did a half-arsed job, and I told him not to use it unless Charlie like it. Charlie said it was "Fackin' brilliant" (his words not mine) but wanted us to redo it but make it as racy (naughty) as possible. We never did!

As Bamby interviewed me one more time I began to feel really faint and realised I'd eaten nothing all day. I'd truly had enough but if I thought that was enough then nothing could prepare me for the actual wedding day which was fast approaching.

Meanwhile Bev was looking all over for me but apparently, she'd smoked so much weed that the hotel staff were following her around with an air freshener as she was making the Italian run hotel smell like a Jamaican weed farm! Bamby told her to stop smoking and they had a row, I went to the hotel staff and apologised and greeted more guests that had arrived and thanked them. Bamby and Bev were still at it and I asked them to stop. Bamby put an end to it and Bev told me to come down to her room. I told her I wanted to stay in the bridal suite as I was bloody knackered, she wasn't pleased but left. Then Bamby and the crew wanted to go out clubbing in Wakefield! "Are you bloody joking?" I said while chomping my way through the complimentary biscuits, "Come on, it's your last night as a single woman." "Yes!" I said, "and I'm spending it in bed!" As it was now approaching midnight, all the lads including Colin could tell from my tone that I'd really had enough. When this girl has had enough, she will make it abundantly clear, 'cos let's face it, it isn't very often. The rest of the party drank more and headed out while I had a shower; I cleansed, and moisturised my face then got in bed and responded to a ton of text messages.

By the time I'd finished I turned off the light and fell asleep. Suddenly, the lads returned, and Colin woke me up; thank God it was only him staying in the room! Anyway, he said they'd had a hell of a night, but he'd fell out with Bamby and almost ended up brawling with him, he said that he had left with the hump and made his way back. Colin immediately got into his side of the king size bed and said: "I can't believe you are really getting married tomorrow… are you nervous?" "Very!" Came my instant response. If only he knew what was about to unfold. And there I laid anxiously pondering for an hour how this would be the very last time I'd be known as Paula Williamson. After weighing up the pro's and con's for a while I slowly drifting off to sleep, in the bizarre knowledge that my future husband, Charlie Bronson-Salvador was only down the road, moments away sleeping soundly in his cage.

Chapter Fourteen: I Do Thee Wed

So, it was the day of my wedding, and for starters, I kicked my body into gear with my much-needed best friend: a cup of Yorkshire tea, this was sweetened with a bit of unrefined sugar for that extra bit of wedding-day zip. Colin, my gay husband housemate told me there were cars suspiciously parked in the cul-de-sac, so immediately I jumped to my feet in my white Hello Kitty dressing gown and peeped through the blinds, making sure I wasn't noticed, and yes, there, in vulture-praying abundance, they were!

At this time every tabloid newspaper wanted a picture of me and catching me looking like the wreck of the Hesperus could be the gold dust they so desperately needed. However, I ain't no fool, and that is something they certainly wouldn't be getting and instead I chose to outsmart them with a little test. I told Colin to take some of the flowers that I'd been sent (made by my beautiful sister-in-law) and drive around the block to see which of the cars followed; they instantly took the bait and sped off giving chase leaving me still staring from the window, chuckling to myself, and then continued getting things in place for when Bamby and the TV crew arrived.

Bamby, (ever the money-maker,) had talked me into making a documentary about it all. I refused at first, but he used his powerful persuasive charm on me by saying that it could really help Charlie, stating that this could be something that may well change the public's perception of him – and for that reason, I obviously agreed. You see for the last month we'd been filming and quite often we clashed heads as I was trying to see the bigger picture and wanted nothing in any piece of film or photo that could make Charlie, or indeed myself, look like a fool.

Bamby wanted a sensationalist documentary, but his methods of how to create such things didn't always sit well with me. One time we'd had a blazing row after interviewing Alan Lord and his partner. Alan was infamous for starting the 1990 Strangeways Prison riots and, after serving 33 years, Alan was now out of prison and happy with his wonderful partner Anita. I wanted to get in an interview with them both to show that with a good partner by your side it could be done, and you could leave the life of extreme incarceration behind its very own door and have a fantastic life with someone you loved.

Alan had his own Gym and Bamby was more interested in chatting, laughing, and playing about on the equipment than doing the interview that I needed for the documentary; an interview that would have hit the right notes and shown the truth to the viewers. At my request, I conducted the interview with Alan and Anita, but it was really rushed and afterwards Bamby went mad saying he was the boss and implied, feeling he'd had his nose pushed out, that I had taken over! I obviously argued my case stating that it was my bloody life not his. As the squabble escalated I demanded he let me out of the car on the M6 so I could walk home without listening to his nonsense. In the end I relented and, since I wasn't allowed to have an opinion about my own bloody life, I simply sat there and refused to speak. To be fair to Bamby he did apologise, but the fact is the man just can't stand things that don't go his way! Bamby, Charlie and I were all hot headed, so perhaps I should've spotted the warning signs a long while back. Anyhow, I was in too deep now and started to get ready, showering, doing my hair and makeup.

I then got a text off my mum and dad which made me cry, I knew this must be hurting them both so much and hated myself for putting them through this but wanted to show everyone that Charlie wasn't how the tabloids made him out to be, but after yesterday's visit and the Bronson incident when I was late I was very worried.

Colin had gone to get me a lovely set of underwear, I thought this was incredibly kind of him and I needed him and was very glad to have him as he cared so much about me. I must confess he was a huge help and support to me during this time, however, he and Bamby clashed. Colin couldn't stand him and never had since the very first moment their paths crossed. True to form, and before we knew it, there was Bamby with a camera in my face at the front door, equipped with all the paraphernalia that comes with filming which included the crew, who thankfully I got on very well with, and in they came and began filming a completely unprepared me.

I told them of the 'paps' that were out in the street and Bamby went straight out to talk to them. To be honest, I saw no harm in them getting a sneaky shot of me putting the stuff into the car. My dress was hidden and that was all they were interested in. I mean, the poor sods had been there for hours, nevertheless, Bamby swiftly got rid of them; I've no idea what he said but they had it away on their toes. Well, all but one, but Bamby made sure I was guarded as I got into the car.

During the commotion, Bev gave me a garter to wear which Flan (Maureen Flanagan) had sent – I appreciated that a lot. Bev then went downstairs to sort things out then promptly informed us that my dress was far too big for the Saab, but it had gone in the Mercedes OK. The paparazzi were there in force trying to get a shot, so to ruin it for them I was bundled into the car under a big purple sheet. To be quite honest, Charlie and I couldn't see the point in hiding my dress! We actually thought, so what if people saw me and the dress? The only official pictures would come from The Mirror, not to mention the exclusive interviews and reception shots, but it wasn't to be and was refused point blank. Looking back, I wished I'd have gone with someone who didn't put so many restraints on the proceedings, but I was so pushed for time and Gemma obviously wanted the exclusive.

Over time, I had confided in Gemma a lot and she never betrayed me re my mental health struggles once. So, although I wanted some freedom, I trusted her at wholeheartedly which was far more important. The fee had to be split with Bamby as he had appointed himself as my agent and took a whopping

50%, which is extremely heavy, because most other agents would only normally take 20%, max. The truth was I couldn't keep up with everything and needed someone's help for a lot of things, this included. Bamby, although a greedy bugger, was exceptionally media savvy.

After going to the visitors building first, one of the paparazzi tried to get into the car and Bev had to smash into him a bit. Having your hair done and then being bundled under a big bloody blanket isn't the best thing for a bride on her wedding day.

Once we arrived, I was swiftly whisked out of the car and bundled inside the prison; the doors closed and rather than little Richie holding my dress up he dropped its train and ended up holding my beautiful flowers that my sister-in-law had done for me, as they were drooping due to the commotion. And suddenly the door slammed shut on Bronson lookalike, Tim Crowley who I had given free rein to speak to the rest of the press to let them know how Charlie was bearing up. Tim said some nice words about the two of us as he had seen us together and knew how in love we were.

Inside, full security checks were respectfully carried out, even though they still had to go through my hair, in a side room. Then Stuart, Charlie's cousin and I stood waiting. I had only just met Stuart the night before, but we had spoken on the phone several times as he was the man who had been chosen to give me away. I was sad my dad wasn't doing it but was grateful for Stuart stepping in.

The walk-in music began to play which was the wrong track; the actual recording we wanted was Hans Zimmer's 'Time', which I had practiced my walk-in to. But no, this was a far slower and more sombre Hans Zimmer tune called 'The Pacific' which wasn't one bit like 'Time'. Anyway, I was confused by this but desperately didn't want to ruin it. I'd told them repeatedly that it was track eight and Charlie had scrubbed out where Rod had put eight and changed it to nine, so, consequently I came in to the wrong piece of music. Which, I might add, wasn't the bloody death march that was printed in the press. Having said that it was sombre enough for anyone's taste. This left me a little downhearted, but as soon as I saw Charlie everything melted away; all of the mishaps in the lead up simply paled into insignificance.

As it happened, the room they had approved for the nuptials was the same one we'd had the parole hearing in, it was a plain room with red plush chairs. This added a bit of colour but was still very prison like. There were no candles or flowers allowed, and we had no decorations at all in the room. Our guests were totally outnumbered by the amount of prison officers present. Round and round in my head I was praying the governor didn't show his face, but then I caught Charlie's face staring at me and his expression was an expression I will have imprinted on my mind forever. This was a surreal moment for me and I imagine even more surreal for Charlie, especially as it was the first time in 20 years, he had worn a suit.

It was now time to say our vows and Charlie immediately tripped while saying my name and then we quickly realised that the ring was tight; the ring was a wonderful design by Adam Croft, but had been made a size too small. Anyway, I didn't push it too far down and for the important moment it fitted. I instantly began to well up, as did Charlie, so I tightened the grip on his hand for reassurance and gave him a cheeky wink to calm him. Then in a heartbeat we had said our vows to one another, signed on the dotted line and that was that… we were married.

A cake with our names on appeared that Charlie had arranged, and after presenting it he did a toast to the governor wishing that he got bollock cancer and that his deputy got arse cancer. I cheered and laughed, a little nervous about what the hell else he may come out with next. We then danced together to Hans Zimmer's 'Time' as everyone applauded in celebration. Charlie is a good mover and more gentile than you'd imagine when he wants to be. He did however tread on the plastic loop thing at the bottom of my dress… but I don't think anybody but me noticed.

We got to sit together kissing and cuddling for a short while, but not as long as we would have hoped. However, we did have time to go through all the photos' and delete the dodgy ones we didn't want. Charlie looked a bit bonkers on some, but I imagine that was simply due to the excitement of the day. Also, there was an alertness about him for the whole two hours which wasn't anything to do with the wedding. Well, apart from when I walked in and when we said the vows… Oh, he was most definitely transfixed on me for those parts. Charlie told me he'd tried to imagine how I would look, but never envisioned what I actually presented him with, and said he honestly didn't know what he'd done to deserve me. In reply I told him he looked really handsome (which he did) and that we were sent to help save one another. I honestly couldn't keep my eyes off him, which was heart-breaking because I knew that our time in that room, together as a newly married couple was about to end abruptly.

When the time came to say goodbye, Charlie took the rest of the cake back with him to share with the segregation block and he and Robert Maudsley (the serial killer who killed four people, three of which fell at his murderous hands in prison) polished it off. When it came to my time to leave, I instantly started to heave and felt like I was going to be sick, but after a minute or two of steady breathing I said: "Okay let's do it people... I am now Mrs. Salvador!" I wanted to leave the prison with a big smile on my face to show everyone, but unfortunately, as soon as my stiletto's hit the cobbles, someone threw a wretched purple blanket over me.

Once out of the car I almost fell over, as my dress was too big so I reached out my arms but they were under the blanket, then I heard a voice guiding me. It was Diane, a friend I had made via Charlie's supporter group, she had been really nice to me and it was such a comfort to me knowing she was there (as it happens her and lookalike Tim got together as a result of the wedding and they now have a gorgeous little boy after sadly losing one before). Oddly enough, people kept saying they were the official Charlie and Paula lookalikes.

In the room a pint of Peroni was given to me by Colin as he knew I would need something refreshing straight away. Cameras flashed as Bamby snapped me. Please not now, let me get ready, I was thinking; I looked bedraggled and was sweating as I was out of breath and needed my makeup and hair touching up. As always, people were in and out of my room, and no sooner had I drank the pint was it coming straight back up and down the toilet and I felt totally dehydrated. At this point the guests had arrived and Bamby was keeping them busy while I had my hair and make-up done while being interviewed. I swiftly sent my mum and dad a text as my phone was going crazy and I knew I wouldn't get another chance for the rest of the day. Then finally it was time to go downstairs, which I did, with Colin on my arm.

There were hundreds of guests… it was packed, and I could barely move. Nevertheless, they made way for me to get to the top table where Ritchie, Colin and Bamby were sat with a dummy of Charlie sitting there with chains on waiting in the seat next to mine. It was bonkers. Bamby was dripping in sweat as he was Master of Ceremonies and although people didn't like his bossiness at least he was helping me sort things out, which was something I struggled to do alone. My mind was racing and all I could think about was my new husband back in his cell all alone. Bamby was more like a compere than an MC, and I was just happy that I had Colin by my side, who knew I needed oodles of prosecco and wine to take on the speeches.

My brother Andrew came in with his two sons and was immediately asked to do a speech. At which point I turned to Bamby and asked: "Bloody hell, how long have I got to come up with something for my speech?" To which he horrifyingly replied: "About 10 minutes Paula!" And I remember thinking, 'crap, now I'm even more nervous.'

I was so pleased my brother came and even more that he stood up and said something, because right at that time he was the only one in the family who was speaking to me. A lot of the people were there for Charlie, those who truly knew him knew how much I had done for him. Dave Courtney (Yellow Pages of British Crime) had called me before to say how much he supported me and all I was doing for Charlie. He also told me to ignore the dickheads as they weren't worth a second of my time. I was extremely pleased to see Dave there, and, ever the talker, he gave a fantastic speech and lifted the atmosphere in the room. And with the tone of the room lifted, I couldn't help myself and jumped from my seat and shouted: "Listen my dears, until the day my husband is free, and living the life he deserves, I will not ever stop campaigning!" Then, I thanked each and everyone of them for being there and said that it meant the absolute world to us, and with a new burst of confidence I carried on for a bit longer as I recognised faces in the crowd that were nodding along in agreement.

While everyone was talking among themselves, Rod put on a recording of Charlies, speaking. The first dance I chose was 'Like A Prayer'. Tim, Charlie's look alike would accompany me, but I hadn't practised. We just went for it. One photo of me leaving that night appeared online and you can almost see my nipple, this was NOT the look I was aiming for, I fell onto the floor in exhaustion at the end whilst dancing with one of my friends Shaun who spun me to the floor. There was lots of clapping, laughter and a great atmosphere. Then everyone queued up to come and congratulate me at the table, it was odd like they were doing a meet and greet but it just happened that way.

I then had to try and make my way to thank everyone but Bamby kept pulling me this way and that way to take photos. He persisted with this until he was literally saying to people, rather abruptly: "You're in, or you're out!" as he had my friends and Charlie's friends queuing up in what looked like a rollcall. All of this just wasn't right, and I really wasn't in the right state of mind for Bamby and his overbearing behaviour.

Feeling extremely pressured by Bamby, I shot off to the ladies and threw up again; a lot of people were coming over to me saying how rude that Bamby bloke was, and how under different circumstances they would have told him straight. However, I pleaded with them not to say anything and said that if they did, he would go off in a mood and I would be left to deal with everything.

I was upset over the photographs, not only did I not have the ones from the service, but also Bamby wasn't taking them properly. I worked for a while with my friend assisting him doing wedding photography, so I knew what was really needed, but whenever I said anything, he just told me to stop whinging. Beverleigh Zacher a wonderful person and friend to myself and Charlie took a picture of me with my brother and my nephews: Bamby immediately saw this and demanded we erased it. "NO!" I insisted. I'm allowed a photo with my family, and apart from a nice one that was taken of me and Tim with the flowers, this is the only photograph I liked from that day. Bev refused to delete it too – Bev doesn't take shit from anybody – Bev could be seen as the intimidator, certainly not the intimidated. I really wish I had one with my other nephew Darren and his girlfriend Kirsty as they were my only other family members there.

As the time was getting on, I changed into the old lady clothes and told Bamby to please let everyone know about the sing-song for Charlie that I'd promised. I went out in full-on cockney character, talking about my grandson who was inside for pinching melons or something daft like that. At which point, I think everybody thought I'd actually lost the bloody plot.

We all got outside the prison for midnight and sang 'What a Wonderful World' as loud as we could so that Charlie could hear it. In the excitement of it all I threw my dress off and was jumping up and down with my knickers, suspenders and stockings on, but still wearing the old lady shoes and wig. I must've looked a right bloody sight. Colin and Bev Straker quickly calmed me down and put a coat over me as I straddled Bev's mobility scooter for the ride back.

Once back, most of the group decided to go off to bed but as there were many people that I had not managed to properly speak to I allowed them to come to our room. These lot stayed late into the early hours. My friend and her date stayed on the chaise longue at the bottom of the bed and started getting up to all-sorts. At which point Colin and I burst out laughing and put pillows over our heads to supress the noise. As things progressed, the female ended up telling him to sod off, so the dirty bugger took himself off to the bathroom to relieve himself.

We woke up next morning and the room was insane; Colin woke and said: "Fuckin' hell, the room looks like it's been raped!" His quip made me laugh as it was a perfect summing up. Our friend Jules, who was a dominatrix had done a life size cardboard stand of herself with poppers in her hand and there were bottles and presents and clothes and bloody everything scattered everywhere.

Bev Straker came in to see if I wanted some food, this was nice of her and she also came up with the reason for the lack of movement in my left leg - I still had the garter on but had slept in such a way it had cut off my circulation. Slowly but surely, we all came round, and my phone started going wild, ringing off the hook. And when I went to open a window for some fresh air Bamby rang straight away and said "Close that bloody curtain ya' daft cow, there is still loads of paparazzi here." Luckily enough, whatever pictures may have been taken never surfaced.

I said goodbye to people discretely at my room as I was still concerned about the 'paps' because I was still being told that no one was allowed to take a picture of me. However, in the end we packed up and said, sod it, they have been waiting for ages, I'm off outside, and with that I went out to the car and I gave them a cheeky, titillating, smile.

Chapter Fifteen: Ticket For One, Please

Charlie insisted that I go on honeymoon alone. I told him that was ridiculous, but he just didn't listen and, as a surprise, he got Bamby to book me one. Mind you, at the time I didn't realise that all these extra things would come from my half of our fee, which was £2000. Bamby was forever bragging how rich he was, so, I naturally assumed he would use part of his 50%, but that wasn't to be. I was so anxious and confused with everything that was going on, and I'm ashamed to say, it all made me a very vulnerable target.

To avoid the hounding paparazzi, once I arrived in Malta Bamby told me to post online that I was still at Gatwick, although we actually flew from East Midlands. When I finally got to my room, I was absolutely exhausted as I had not stopped at all for months, and despite my use of sleeping aids I was barely sleeping and was taking more and more to combat it. I knew I'd need my diazepam on holiday but couldn't take them with me as they weren't prescribed meds, they were knock-off ones that I used to discretely purchase from eBay and certain pharmacy companies online.

On route to the airport Bamby with his laptop out sent the pics to the Mirror. We had agreed beforehand that he would let me proof them before he sent them so at least I'd have some control. I was always worried about the pictures because sometime earlier the Mirror had published a pic of me looking a lot bigger than I was and Charlie had gone mad saying I looked like I had eaten a horse, cheeky beggar. I laughed it off at the time, but that photo and comment made me forever conscious about my size and I was very aware of looking fat in pics as I'm naturally curvaceous and can easily look bigger than I actually am. However, Bamby went back on his word and said they had already been sent! Bamby had gone against my original wishes and he bloody knew it; he knew that it would annoy me and could be devastating for me, but he just didn't give a shit and said: "Stop being a fucking drama queen, Paula!" My blood was boiling, but I decided to forget it and focus my mind on the sun shining in Malta.

As it happened there was only one day of bloody sunshine... bloody typical! Yeh, that's right, even the sun had the hump when I was around. Having said that, it didn't matter to me because I had sunken into a deep depression and barely came out of my room. Nevertheless, Bamby with his cheerfully motivating attitude managed to convince me to go down for dinner and drinks. For me though the fuel for the body's survival was of no consequence 'cos when I was down and depressed it was always about the drinks, and because this place was all inclusive, I could simply drink and relax myself into unconsciousness to escape. And this I hoped would settle my mind and push the negative thoughts from it. I was now drinking on a daily basis and the all-inclusive element of the holiday meant that from bar to hotel room I could have a continuous flow of vino.

I had always wondered about Charlie's first wife Irene and had asked Charlie many times about her and their son Mike. He told me she had originally lied to Mike saying his dad was dead but then they met inside prison when Mike was also serving some time. I have the photo of Charlie holding his now grown up son with that long beard he had. But in regard to Irene, apart from telling me she had left him, divorced him and lied about him being dead he told me she was a nice-looking woman.

I had always been fascinated by her and wondered how she had moved on with her life. Soon after, the news came that she was going to be appearing on This Morning for ITV. Bamby said his friend at ITV had said she wasn't going to paint a very good picture of Charlie, but he had managed to get word to him to speak to her and ask her to be a little kinder than she had planned, especially considering I had just married him.

I was desperate to watch the interview, but couldn't get it to play on my phone, so my good friend Beverleigh Zacher recorded it on her phone and sent it to me over the messaging app, WhatsApp. My first impression was how fabulous she looked; I loved her black hair, her outfit, and pink boots, she was lovely and didn't say a bad word about Charlie. She also wished me luck, which was kind of her and I hoped we could meet again at some point.

One day Bamby called my room to say he was going for lunch and to come with him if I wanted, when I got this I got this god awful pain in my chest, I could barely move or breathe I thought I was having a bloody heart attack, so I emailed Charlie to tell him about the pain; I was topless when it happened and I couldn't move or be arsed to get dressed. Suddenly, a cleaner came into my room, my saviour, well that's what I'd hoped, however, when she saw me clutching my chest and gasping for air, she just left the room all embarrassed. I honestly thought my time was up. It lasted for several hours until I finally began to breathe. Charlie called me and told me I had had a full-on panic attack and that he had them too and that's why he knew the symptoms. He must have used a lot of his units to call but said that he wasn't bothered and that he wanted to make sure I was okay. He asked if I was doing as I was told and enjoying myself? I lied a little, not telling him that I had spent every day except one alone in my room in bed.

The one time I did venture out is when the photo was snapped by the Daily Star, and a few more online papers of me where I put the book of Charlies face over my crotch as I sunbathed. I did that on purpose for Charlie so that he would get a sample. Somehow, I never ended up with the money for that either. As we arrived at the airport for the return flight home there I was splashed right across the front page. It was a photo of me and Tim Crowley dancing – I looked absolutely terrible. There were other shots that were far better but apparently, as always, Bamby knew best! Well he certainly didn't with that bloody one 'cos I looked like I was chewing a wasp whilst sashaying the night away. Anyway, inevitably the phone was ringing off-the-hook again.

Some man on the plane home recognised me and wished me all the best, which was very kind. Mind you, I did notice several others on the plane reading the damning article about me, so I put my cap on, pulled it down over my eyes and tried to stay incognito for the whole journey. I wasn't ready for any negativity. I was in no fit state to take on the scolding masses as I was feeling totally depressed.

As soon as we arrived home, Bamby informed me that he had arranged an interview for me on the Lorraine Kelly show of the same name. I never even got time to go home first! Lorraine was absolutely lovely to me and gave me a pair of tights to wear as I was paranoid about my legs, she really reassured me and could see that I was far quieter than I had been on Loose Women and GMB.

Bamby was his usual self and was very bloody loud, he even said: "Here she is… she's a nutter! But hey, she is getting paid x amounts of pounds." This remark obviously made it look like I had married Charlie simply to get rich; I'm not a fool, as if I would marry him to get rich, I mean I've dated many monied men in my time. I could have married a millionaire easy and had had an offer prior to Charlie. Nevertheless, I had picked Charlie for simply being Charlie - bloody hell, if my manager was broadcasting to the masses that I was a gold-digger, what bloody hope did I have. I wished he could have just taken the time to notice that I was slipping. I mean, I was extremely nervous before I went on the show, was this man bloody blind or something. Anyway, as I said previously, fortunately for me and my butterflies Lorraine was as kind-hearted and empathetic as I'd imagined, and she also wished me all the best after the interview and gave me a reassuring kiss, bless her.

I'm glad I was able to talk about Charlie and me on the TV; having the platform to talk openly about our relationship without having to deal with any confrontation was so uplifting and refreshing. Oh, of course the onslaught of negativity comments weren't too far away, but I personally had so many sup-porters and friends assuring me that I had done a good interview and that I had conducted myself superbly.

We had some more radio interviews booked in but the negativity and the way I was being pushed about was getting to me. This is just Bamby's way, he does make me laugh but he is also extremely exhausting and when we went back to the hotel for breakfast, he immediately went off to take a call. At this point Rod rang. I was already crying so he put his wife Linda on the phone, and she began asking what had happened and I emphasised to her that I needed to go home and that I was mentally drained! I went on to say that I was trying my utmost to keep upbeat for Charlie but didn't feel right and that Bamby was throwing all sorts of radio interviews at me. Linda insisted that I wasn't to do anything I didn't want to do; strangely echoing the words of Bamby when I called him before my marriage when I met Charlie. I went on to say to Linda that I was on auto pilot but drowning very quickly.

Shortly after Bamby came back, at first, he never noticed me crying, but then asked me what was up, and I reiterated the points I'd been making to Linda: telling him that I was mentally drained and not just from the wedding but from all I have to sort out with the constant messages etc. Moreover, I was still up until the early hours replying to tons of messages, because If I didn't, they would build up to hundreds and hundreds. I also told him that I wanted to see my mum, dad, Colin, and my bloody cats for some comfort. I mean, I hadn't stopped since I told him on the phone that I accepted Charlie's proposal. I was heading for mental breakdown, not for marrying Charlie, but by the way I was being paraded as some kind of business tool.

For the first interview, due to my eyes being really swelled up from crying, I wore a cap and sunglasses as I didn't want anybody to see. The presenter was pretty judgemental and as usual the same old questions were asked. Bamby immediately stepped in to back me up because he could see I was quietly having a break down, but the only problem was, while being overly assertive, he came across very aggressive; that man certainly does speak from the hip with passion - always saying it like it is. Well off-air I didn't mind him including himself, 'cos he was just sticking up for me, but on air was a different story altogether and during a little break the interviewer went a little nuts and said: "Look, I do fucking mind you interjecting! You're arrogant and you're trying to bully me on my own fucking show, now get out both of you! OUT!" She hollered, while instructing the security to get the two of us out of the building. She wasn't bloody happy! And to be honest I didn't know whether to laugh or cry and so unenthusiastically laughed along with Bamby. I was a little angry and felt that I had cried quite enough: it's not great getting kicked off a show, but she was pretty rude and judgemental and clearly couldn't take it as well as give it! And all this despite my trying my best to keep the bloody peace.

I would always ask Rod's advice when I did anything; I wanted to know that I had represented Charlie well. He texted George to say it was done well, and he text me to say it was heated. Not too many of our lot got to hear it which I was pleased about. Anyway, I arrived back home, albeit with a new case that had to be bought because in the rush I had used Bamby's suitcase to put my things in for Malta. But for now, I was home, back to a little normality, so glad to see Colin and my best pals, the cats, and with a sigh of relief, I collapsed.

Another interview Bamby had set up for me was with the journalist from the Daily Mail: this was a female who had contacted me personally to do a follow up story. This too was such a strained interview! This girl by the name of Natalie was asking me questions and when I was halfway through my answer Bamby would abruptly interject. For example: he said we were making the first documentary ever with Charlie actually on camera, so I jumped in and politely disagreed with him: "No he isn't in it, he is not allowed to do any media!" At which point Bamby rolled his eyes at me to make me go along with his story. In regard to this sort of thing Bamby was clueless. I mean, it was a lie and furthermore it could have caused further damage to Charlie and his potential progression. Moreover, the tabloids would've had a field day printing it, because God only knows what further security measures might have been put in place as a result. It could have effectively stopped certain visits… and not just my ones. For Charlie's sake and mine I really had to argue our case. Natalie had to intervene and say this was my interview and as such she only needed to speak to me, so Bamby immediately went off in a huff. I'm no liar and told Natalie that the text my mum had sent on the day had said to send their love to Charlie. I desperately felt that I needed to paint a picture that my mum wasn't horrifically opposed to our wedding, because if that got out, she would have had more journalists camped outside her house. Then my mum would've reacted to the press and would have ended up splashed all over the front bloody page of the nationals. As I'm sure you can imagine, I was trying to keep everything as amicable as possible for everyone involved; however, unbeknown to me at that time, for the next 18 months my embellishment of that text was to cause me no end of trouble and anxiety: I had simply made an innocent comment but to my mum it was horrific! I could see her point which I will touch on a little later.

After the interview I had my hair and makeup done to look good for the article. Although, they used an old photograph of Tim Crowley (Bronson lookalike) and me, instead of the ones from the actual shoot. I thought Natalie had done a great job, as did Gemma who always got me copy approval. (copy approval is when you get to look over the text and or photographs before a piece goes to print). However, she called Bamby in Malta saying that they were almost going to pull the story as they had Gemma's dictaphone recording, this was the one Bamby had left when he wanted to deal with The Sun. I'd told him it was a bad idea and that's why I was so insistent that she erased it and start again but Bamby was rushing me and at the time I knew we could've very easily lost it.

I'm too honest for this business. I guess I was simply a girl who had fallen for someone and was fighting for him to be accepted as the man he was today and not the man with a plethora of detrimental misdemeanours. My plan was not for him to be released immediately; it was just to know that he was heading in the right direction. So, my way was to always play fair with everyone. This was no easy task as it was hard pleasing Charlie, Bamby and Rod as one entity. You see, my concern was for Charlie, which unbeknown to me, and once I'd realised what I had done, was soon to be replaced by concern for my family.

Once home, I received a call from my dad saying that my mum was very upset with the story that was in the Mail on Sunday, and said I needed to go and see her. He also said that I should treat the situation a little delicately and with caution 'cos she was furious! So anyway, I said that I'd be with her in half hour. To be honest, I was still knackered but went straight round. When I arrived, my mum could barely look at me but then she quickly opened up and asked why there were lies in the paper. Mum went on to say that she didn't have control of what I said but that she was extremely upset at the comment I made about the text she sent and asked why I'd said they wanted to send their

love to Charlie. Mum said "Because darling, I didn't say that." I immediately
put my case forward and said that I was sorry and that I had done it for Charlie
because he just wanted to speak with mum, and that if she'd spoken with him, I
know that she would warm to him.

In the past, when I had been in a phone conversation with Charlie,
I had passed the phone to her several times and she had spoken briefly but
handed the phone back as quickly as she could. I also told mum that the press
had been asking how she was and how she felt about the situation etc. I went
on to say to mum that if I had told the tabloids the actual truth, the entire story
would have been focused on that and nothing else. I said: "Mum, you know how
the papers love to concentrate on the negatives and nothing else." Mind you,
I was finally beginning to see how newspapers work and what they want; my
mum was offered a very substantial amount of money - enough to really benefit
her, but she is a very proud lady and has always said no. I finished off by saying
that if the article was focused on that negative re her and Charlie the papers
would hound her again; I did stretch the truth a little to simply bypass that, in the
hope of not hurting Charlie.

I must confess that during the furore I honestly hadn't seen how much
it was affecting my mum. And almost overnight she developed extreme anxiety
and bouts of depression. My mum is one of the strongest women I have ever
known, but my stupidity had pushed her over the edge; the daughter she waited
20 years to come along had done this to her. Suddenly, my mum's appetite
ceased, because apparently due to her extreme anxiety she was worried about
choking to death. Thanks to one of my brothers we managed to get mum to
see a private doctor and they discovered a slight kink in her gullet, which had
probably been there for years. I tried to offer help by taking her to the appoint-
ments. However, her health continued to deteriorate, she was shrinking in size
and before we knew it, Mum had lost half her body weight – due, in part I guess,
to the medication she was taking.

One evening mum had a combined asthma attack (that had got worse)
and a panic attack, and an ambulance had to be called; the paramedic came
and calmed her down, saying: "There you are Mrs. Williamson, mind you it
could be worse, I mean you could be the mother of that girl who just married
that Charlie Bronson!" I kid you not, those were his exact words. Then of course
with him saying that it set Mum off again. I was distraught, my actions had
caused my lovely mum so much torment.

That article had pushed her over the edge, and it was all my bloody
fault. People called her asking her if it was true that she was sending love and
blessings to Charlie and me. So, to set the record straight: I have never had
my mum's blessing, my dad was less harsh about it but still wished I could've
fallen for someone who could have look after me in the 'normal' way. I'm forever
telling my dad that it's not the 1800s and that I knew what I was doing, but to
him in a lot of ways I was still his little girl. Furthermore, both of my parents are

acutely aware of my mental frailty, and simply want me to be well and above all, be happy.

I'm pleased to say that me and my mum worked through our differences and are closer now than ever. What is more, I will never hurt her again and will forever be sorry for putting her through anything like that. I'm sure if she met Charlie outside of prison she would find him funny – mind you, she wouldn't like his bad bloody language. Having said that, I honestly think Charlie would have adapted a touch of decorum, well he certainly did when in his own mum's company and his mum and mine, in many ways, are very similar. My mum certainly would've got on with Charlie's mum, I'm sure. Furthermore, in conversations with my mum and dad they have both said that Irene sounded like a lovely lady - which she is.

Chapter Sixteen: The Accidental Whipping Boy

Christmas came and went; mum still couldn't eat and had a panic attack over a brussel sprout on Christmas day, her birthday, so unfortunately we had to take her home. January hit, and I settled back into my secretarial type duties. We had heard back from the parole hearing which all seemed extremely positive and I could see a move for Charlie, possibly to Strangeways or Woodhill in Milton Keynes. We were also fighting for the right to be given our wedding photographs: Charlie wanted his and my mum to have a set, of which I had already got the folders. By this point I was working very closely with his legal team, speaking frequently with John, Charlie's solicitor, and Rod and Bamby, although he had been busy with the museum too.

On the 26th January I got a call from HMP Frankland in Durham. They had Charlie and wanted me to know that he was okay. They said he was fine and that he had requested them to call me. They said he was fine and that he had requested for to them to call me. I spoke to John who informed me that there had been an incident with Mark Doherty the Segregation Governor, and because of this Charlie had been ghosted out up to Frankland. Charlie wrote and confirmed that there had been a bit of incident with the Governor and this was the reason he had been transferred.

Soon after, when the time was right, I visited him. Thankfully two supporters, Paula, and Julian who I had met for the protest up in London had kept in touch, they were a lovely couple, who said they were happy for Tim Price and I to stay with them at their house when we were up for a visit. Tim wasn't on the first visit because Charlie just wanted to see me alone. This was an open visit, which was a new experience for me - totally different to Wakefield. I was very pleased it was an open prison because we got to hug and kiss one another, we even had a little dance (no music: just the sweet clatter gate-keys as seven guards stood gazing at us).

Fortunately, now that Charlie was in Frankland, I told him I could manage a visit every other week, but not every week as it was too much. I would stay with Paula and Julian for the two nights while I was in Durham, which was lucky because 'taking everything into account' without room and board I would easily spend hundred quid on a visit which I could ill afford.

On my second visit to Frankland Charlie looked considerably worse, he looked stressed and his eyes weren't right; he told me that he had been storing his butter which concerned me because butter and boot-polish have been defensive tools he has used in the past to smother himself in when he is about to kick off. I told him to not do anything stupid as he was already in trouble for what had happened at Wakefield. However, he told me that I had to understand that my world was completely different to his and said that this place wasn't good for him mentally. I could see what he meant, as the place had an air of absolute doom about it. Charlie had been here before (he's been in almost every prison), but this time really was not a good time for him to be there.

On Valentine's day, a year since our proposal, he stripped off in the yard took out the Lurpak, and started buttering himself up and shouted over to the guard: "Oi mate you better call for back up because there is about to be a rumble?" Then with that he got himself livened up and just waited until sixteen armed guards arrived and then ploughed into them all. Charlie floored a good few of 'em but was soon overpowered and taken to the floor which has permanently messed up his right shoulder. He wrote and told me that he had wanted to see me on Valentine's day; but unfortunately it fell on a day that was a non-visit day. However, I know it was an excuse because he wanted a rumble – A 'Valentine's day massacre', as he called it, nevertheless, it was Charlie who got massacred; mind you, at least that place hadn't ruined his dark sense of humour, but it was messing with his mind.

So, bouts of violence came in abundance, which was perfect negative writing artillery for the media; what could I say? I was a little stunned myself. Now, I could understand if someone had had a go at him and he had fought back in defence, but these were deliberate acts of violence, on his part, not to mention a short time after another violent incident which happened at that place. Charlie may have felt it in that hole, but I was the one receiving all the flak from it on the outside. I was the one with the task of calling his mum and try to explain to her that her son was okay when I knew he obviously wasn't.

At this point in the Bronson and me saga I had met Irene, Charlies first wife and we got on like a house on fire; we were like sisters and had even gone on Loose Women together in aid of Charlie's cause. Charlie was happy we were friends, and she was the only person I could truly relate to. She was the only one who could empathise regarding what I was going through as she had been through it 40 years earlier. Irene and I giggled our time away on Loose Women, that's simply how we are whenever we're together. However, obviously I got loads of criticism for it. For the record, and for anybody out there stupid enough to think I do, I don't and never would condone Charlie's acts of violence.

I had asked to have Paula and Julian passed for a visit with Charlie, as they wanted to thank him for the gifts etc he'd sent them. After which I fell into depression, so much so that it was even hard being in my own home.

Charlie suggested I have a holiday as Harry Holland who runs the market stalls on EastEnders had said I could use his villa that he had in Tenerife. I said to Colin I would take him as a thank you for helping me with the wedding and sticking by me. Unfortunately, Colin's passport hadn't come through and I had to go alone with Colin saying he would come out to me as soon as it arrived. I had never flown alone before and felt really pleased with myself once I got there. And once I'd arrived at the villa safe, I called Harry and told him.

So, a few days passed in Tenerife: I cooked, read, swam, and sunbathed, and had a little exploration on my lonesome. For a short time, I wanted to be alone and didn't even invite conversation. I did like the place but wished that Colin could join me. I had a drink with Pete, a friend of Frances Shea's: Frances is the niece of Reggie Krays late wife of the same name.

Colin arrived about halfway through the holiday and he and I were ridiculously excited. With no time to waste Colin sorted my hair and we immediately hit the town. We then had a drink with Pete, before heading to gaysville, aka Veronica Strip in Playa d' las Americas so we could dance the night away and have fun. Colin was on fine form. Strangely enough, I had felt sick in the day and didn't want to go. It felt as though something was telling me not to go out but because Colin had turned up I felt it my duty.

During the evening, we chatted with lots of different people; finally speaking to some lads from North London who knew the gay strip very well. So, once it was open, we all ventured into the bars' and began knocking back shot after shot and dancing our heads off.

I don't normally tell people anything about Charlie because I often find that once they know then it's all they want to talk about. On reflection, I didn't have my ring on as my fingers were swollen and the ring felt too tight: sometimes if it's hot it would feel very tight, like it's a size too small. The lads were having a laugh, no one tried it on with me, but because my boobs were on show with the dress I had on, one of the lads asked if my boobs were real. "Of course they're real you cheeky sod!" I told him as I began jiggling and laughing. With that he put his hands on them and we all began laughing and carried on dancing. Later that evening Robbie my college mate text me to say, "Paula you have had a gay man's hands in your boobs!" A little later, as we posed for a selfie one of the lads kissed my cheek then we parted company as Colin and I went off to another bar, then an hour or so later went back to the villa. For the record, aside from Colin, me, and the resident cleaner, not another soul came in the villa.

The following day Colin and I were both absolutely shattered, but I mustered up enough energy to laugh at Colin with his legs resting on my suitcase announcing that his dancing days were over! "Yeah right" I said, while laughing. Anyway, for the rest of the holiday we stayed pretty local with no more nights out - just the two of us enjoying wine and meals in the relaxed atmosphere of the odd restaurant. I messaged Charlie and Harry Holland to let them know I was back and thanked Harry once again for allowing me to use his villa.

We got back in the middle of the night and I was shattered from driving, although I still had things to unpack when Mark, my manager from JCM Management called (I had acquired a new manager now) to say apparently the Sun newspaper were running a story on me being in a motorboat incident being rather naughty. Well, at least those were the words I heard, to which I replied: "Well it definitely wasn't me because I haven't even been on a motorboat and don't know what you are talking about?" Mark then explained that being motor-boated is the act of somebody sticking their head between your cleavage and wiggling it from side-to-side. Oh, for goodness sake I thought, this has most definitely been blown way out of all proportion. Nevertheless, I wasn't at all worried because Charlie loves other men fancying me and isn't jealous one bit.

In fact, it's quite the opposite, as Charlie's fantasy was the idea of loads of men wanking themselves off over me so I hardly thought this would upset him. However, on this occasion I could not be more wrong!

Apparently, back home at Frankland prison they had cut it out of the paper, so they knew it was something to do with Charlie, especially as I sent him an email telling him immediately about the facts of the situation; telling him that it was just a group of gay lads on holiday being silly. I went on to say that if I thought for one moment it would upset Charlie, I wouldn't have dreamt of allowing it to happen, but as I say, Charlie knows I'm a flirt and that I always feel safe with gay men. Well, all hell broke loose and soon all the tabloids picked it up, only that day earlier in Tenerife Jane Moore had written in her article about me, I had to get a copy, it said about Charlie's recent offences and had a photo of me sticking my tongue out to the paparazzi with my thumbs up. Jane ended the column saying gives a whole new meaning to the term 'blushing bride!' She had a point because Charlie had committed violent offences that resulted in him being stuck in a cold cell; he would sleep on the floor (by choice) as he said that the mattress was far too lumpy, he also refused a table and chairs and he just had a toilet and sink but we all know all of this wasn't doing himself any favours.

I was deeply sorry as I knew the damning photograph would humiliate him. I also had to explain to Harry about it, but the pic was awful and had been taken completely out of context. I wrote Charlie a letter explaining how sorry I was, but hey, he had been no angel himself either and for something as silly and innocent as this you don't just bail. Rod called me explaining how furious Charlie was; I begged Charlie to let me visit but he was simply having none of it. The next day I got a call from John, Charlie solicitor saying: "Paula I hate having to do this and I can't get involved personally as I have to carry out Charlies instructions but you have done so much for him, and I am sorry but he is going to file for a divorce! He has made up his mind and there is no turning back."

I could barely get my words out through the tears, but I managed to thank him for all he had done for Charlie and wished him all the best... but then I just couldn't speak and put the phone down. I was literally in the same spot where I collapsed when Emma left me, and now, without even giving me the chance to talk it over with him, Charlie was dumping me. I had stood by him when he repeatedly committed a mass of offences, and he's throwing it all away over a one-off silly incident with a bunch of lads who just happen to be bloody GAY! – but was that really the truth? I mean how could a man who liked the idea of prisoners whacking themselves off over pictures of me be upset by men who have no interest in women whatsoever stick their head between my boobs – it makes no sense at all to me.

Anyway, what was done was done and my whole world came crashing down around me. Charlie wouldn't even see me, and I was now being erased like so many others before me. Just 72 hours after John telling me Charlie was going to file for divorce another dark-haired woman was being sucked in by him.

This one was Simon Cowells ex Jasmine Lennard, and not only was he writing to her, but she was sharing what he was writing on social media, and then for some reason she began to cyber bully me herself - calling me dreadful names and mocking me. I never once responded to her – my friend Bev Zacher did, and I wanted to, but my manager had impressed upon me not to react.

This Jasmine girl also shared a photograph of herself posing, and Charlie had written around it using the exact same words he used endearingly with me. No one said a thing to her, and all her followers were encouraging her to go for it. But this man was still my husband as no legal papers had ever come to me and no further discussions of divorce were ever mentioned. There was a very cruel thing she put on a piece of artwork by Charlie and she had put a derogatory and very humiliating comment about my weight; it hurt like hell and was like a punch to the stomach. Both of them mocking me really hurt, further-more, this idiot Jasmine really hadn't a clue what she was spouting – she never even bothered to get the facts right.

Jasmine mocked me so much that my (our) wonderful friend Jules put her in her place, although I did write to Charlie saying I'd accepted he had moved on (even that quick) but all this woman was known for was being Simon Cowell's ex; a bitch and a cokehead, chain smoker who seeks fame and lives off a sugar daddy in the Bahamas.

Charlie tried to convince me that I was wrong, saying that she was a sweet woman but there was nothing in it anyway. As it turned out, they never met and Charlie soon found out she wouldn't have put the work in like the real people in his life and that she was simply using his name as a platform. I would have loved to have been a fly on the wall if they ever met – it would have been a site to behold, all six stone of her towering over him. I watched some her YouTube bits from Big Brother, and she was absolutely vile! I had heard that a few people had tried to warn Charlie away from her but in the end, he got rid of her and her name is dirt – it's a shame he never listened to me from the start though.

The whole debacle had made me a nervous wreck, and I turned more and more to drink, and my addiction to benzos was getting dangerously high. One day I thought, after all I had done, and the upset I had apparently caused him, I thought, I'm not right in the head and shouldn't be here, and so took yet another overdose. I passed out but woke up on my floor hours and hours later - I must be bloody indestructible. I was very shaky for a while and kept crying and crying over Charlie.

Then an article came out which stated that Charlie had slagged me off, this wasn't his style and I immediately knew who was behind it. The Star on Sunday texted me (as one of their journalists had my number) and wanted to know if I wanted to reply. She said that I had a right to after being so publicly humiliated. However, I said I wasn't sure, so she just asked me a few questions via text messages. One of the questions was "I bet you're glad you never got to have sex with him, aren't you?" To which I replied, "No I'm not glad at all … I wanted my husband in every way and still do, but it is what it is!" She then asked: "So what does he look like now, has he changed?" And I told her I didn't know, because I hadn't seen him since my last visit which was in June and that was when I took Paula and Julian in so they could meet him. I really wish I had some memories of that last visit we had alone. But we weren't to know what was going to happen, were we?

I told her that he probably looked a bit more withdrawn, due to the fact that he is now vegetarian and Frankland are not making any provisions for his dietary needs – which is all wrong considering how hard he trains every day. I did mention the boob incident because yes, I was angry! And yes, I also mentioned what people send him and how ungrateful he can be if it's what he classes as measly. I mean, no one sends me all this money and I'm the one on the outside paying all the bloody bills etc and doing all the work. However, I gave her strict instructions not to print anything until I had had chance to think about it more as I told her that she had caught me at a time when I was very hurt and extremely humiliated.

Of course, the Facebook cyber bullying group went to town on me in full flight. Talk about kick a dog when it's down, some really vile people with even more vile mouths, but also some wonderful people commented, too. A lot of women were now contacting me asking how I was, some were hoping the two of us could show the world that we deserved a future, but also said that in light of the Jasmine Lennard saga they had lost all respect for Charlie. Jasmine also publicly thanked Rod for sending the roses and chocolates to her on behalf of Charlie.

A few months previously I had been asked to do a talk in Manchester about my husband, I was approached by a company to do this talk, Charlie loved the idea. I'm crap with technology but with the help of my friend Gareth we painstakingly created the different pages for the talk using Powerpoint. I was incredibly nervous, but Colin came for support as did Paula and Julian and Craig from all the way up in Durham. It's strange but no matter how many of these things I did was always so terrified and nervous; I never got nervous like this with my acting work, but this was a little different – this wasn't a part I could hide myself in.

Anyway, I needed to know all I could about his offences, and the law and prison system; it was almost like studying for a degree, and I was forever asking Rod as he knows such a lot because his life revolves around Charlie and has done some 7 or so years. I had worked with Rod ever so closely, I knew how important he was to Charlie and did everything in my power to be as helpful as I could for him. Rod never had to ask for anything twice and we would spend hours on the phone sorting things out.

Charlie's other wife, Lorraine, on the other hand couldn't stand Rod, she wanted no one around Charlie. I wanted as many good decent supporters and people in his life as I could get; I was never possessive or jealous, I knew he probably sent cheeky letters to women, in the same way that I flirted with men, but we both knew this of each other. And there was Rod carrying out Charlie's commands, never once saying how bad it would portray Charlie in the public eye as this Jasmine stupidly posted everything to Twitter.

For many years, most people weren't even aware of my correspondence with Charlie, that's the difference. The arseholes chose to bully me because I was vulnerable. I had also been extremely open about my mental illness, so to see one of the comments that was actually ridiculing me saying "I hope she is suffering now, the stupid fat bitch" accompanied by a less than flattering, slightly overweight photo of me that had appeared in the media. I barely left my house. Getting out of bed was an effort each day and I was drinking and taking pills more and more. I would make my 'Paula Cocktails', which consisted of loads of powder emptied from various benzos into a fizzy drink such as prosecco and it would affect my speech a lot and my cognitive functions. Still, I didn't care - as long as my cats were fed and looked after, to be quite truthful, I couldn't give a crap.

It became increasingly more difficult living with Colin. I think he found me lazy, but I had severe depression. He would blow all his wages (when he actually turned up for work) on God knows what, but I was forever chasing him for the rent. When it came to the rent it would be excuse after excuse, he was a bloody nightmare. Oh, not to mention the fact that he had also broken a few things around the house but took no responsibility for them whatsoever. Very quickly I began to realise the only time we got on was when we were off our heads. And all the other times I'd spend in tears over it all.

An offer came in and I accepted it as I wanted to apologise to Charlie, his family (his mum especially) and my family for the photos of me that were splashed across the tabloids. I knew they had asked Charlie for a right to reply and they had it cued up for the show. I was so determined to be strong, and wanted to stress that yes, due to the way it had turned out for Charlie and me I was there to eat humble pie. I held Jane Moore's hand and thanked her for warning me, Nadia Sawalha said the situation was ridiculous and that this kind of thing was what a lot of women do for a laugh when they're on holiday and that it was obvious to her that there was nothing except jollity in it. I must say, I was pleased to see Kelly Osbourne on the panel as I had watched the day before when she had been speaking in length about the effects of benzo abuse. Charlie's statement was read out and I couldn't stop crying. He said I was an angel, but I had an alcohol and prescription drug problem that changes my personality and makes me do crazy things. Well, that was that, because now the whole nation including my family were privy to my drug problems.

Kelly Osbourne put her hand on me for reassurance, and when I admitted to what had been said in Charlie's statement the women seemed concerned. They had watched as the smiley, bubbly, slim, dark-haired young woman from my first appearance had now turned into an overweight, frightened, shaking woman who had admitted that she had turned to alcohol and drugs for solace. Put anyone through this without BPD and all that comes with it and see how they would cope; I loved Charlie and still do and probably always will, but all this seemed to be driving me back to a psychiatric hospital - it really was. However, the team at Loose Women were brilliant.

I spoke to the researcher the day before and couldn't stop crying and he asked me if I wanted to cancel, to which I said: "No, I am committed to you and the show, so I will still do it! I need to!" And if I'm to be honest, thank God I did. As soon as we stopped filming my head hit the table and I was in absolute fits of tears. I caught a brief glimpse of the audience and mouthed to them that I was sorry – I imagine they got a little bit more from the show than they had originally expected. Which is amazing for the show's viewers, but certainly not for me and my increasing state of anguish.

As I glanced across the room, most of the faces I saw were those of concern and worry not the hard-judgemental faces of my past times on the show. The team asked me to wait in my dressing room for their in-house councillor, Penny to see me. I finished talking to Kelly who was lovely (I have always admired Kelly and her mum, and her mum interviewed one of my pin-up idols Anna Nicole Smith. I'm forever drawn to these strong yet very vulnerable women because I seem to identify with them. And although many will laugh at this, I even think Anna is one of my guardian angels, I really do!) Moreover, I have proof, which I will tell you about later.

Penny, who is friends and has contacts with the Amy Winehouse Foundation, was wonderful and extremely helpful. (Amy is another iconic figure I feel I have an affinity with, I think it is down to her dedication to love and I identify with the way she totally dedicates herself to it): The two of us make lots of bad decisions at times but we're not bad people. I stayed with Penny for two hours and then went to the pub. Later, I texted her to thank her and to honestly say how desperate I had become and that I desperately needed help. Penny must have immediately got on the case for me, because in no time I was contacted by a lovely man from the Amy Winehouse Foundation; we spoke for a long time, and he mentioned rehab! Eek! I was petrified!

Initially, I was worried about leaving the house and cats in Colin's hands, because once he has taken whatever substances are his choice of the day, he can be a bit of a Jekyll and Hyde and there is simply no way of helping him. Not to mention the anxiety running through my head of just who he might decide to bring back to my house. Fortunately, my mum and dad said they would call to the house and make sure everything was okay. That reassured me a little. Nevertheless, before all of this could take place, I apparently needed to be assessed at my home.

The day of the visit came and for some reason I was extremely anxious. Furthermore, I had not cleaned the house properly, but I just couldn't pull myself out of bed to do it. Plus, the fact that even when I did manage to get up, I was then confronted with the task of deciding what to bloody wear. However, once I had urged myself from slumber and dragged my body downstairs, to my annoyance, I realised that the only alcohol I had in the house was vodka, and I don't usually drink vodka at home. Now, I know that sounds a little odd but I'm just an odd kinda' gal. However, needs-must so as well as my routine breakfast of an array of prescription pills to steady my nerves, I poured myself a small glass of vodka.

In the end I couldn't even get dressed, I was still in my dressing gown, no makeup, hair unwashed I was completely embarrassed; to think how I was only a year or two ago – the woman I was then and the woman I was that day would seem polar opposites to anybody looking in. They obviously didn't judge me because I imagine they had seen far worse. They told me I was an addict, and that it wasn't something to be ashamed of. Nevertheless they did emphasise the severity of my addiction and informed me that I required immediate and abrupt residential rehab attention.

The next day I got a call to say that hopefully there would be a bed available in a few weeks time and that someone from Clouds House would call to verify; to be honest, they called many times, different people that played different roles, apparently they needed accurate information and that's why I was interviewed by an excess of so called experts. I had to contribute towards the cost, but the rest was paid for. I was so thankful and could not stop crying, but as always, I knew that I probably still had a long wait on my hands. The way it works is this: If another person with more severe issues came along then the wait would be longer or worse still, I would have to seek out a different rehab facility. I'm by no means selfish and completely understood – however, the next thing you know they called stating that a bed was ready for me and I would have 6 weeks to get myself well and clean.

If I'm honest, I had no idea what went on behind the walls of rehab; other than being taken off drink and drugs, but to be honest the idea of not being able to have wine was tipping me over the edge. However, and as a result of my addiction I had piled on weight and was in desperate need of a short sharp shock. My agent Mark said he would drive me down with his assistant, so I said my goodbyes to the people closest to me. And until I told my dad that this place could potentially save my life, he really couldn't understand it at all - I think he always buried his head in the sand. I felt terrible was putting my parents through all of this, but I simply had no other choice.

Then, to make things worse a story went in the tabloids about me. This I really couldn't deal with, so I asked my manager Mark at JCM Management to take my phone with him; mind you at this point I was under the impression that such items for outside communication were strictly forbidden in rehab. Although, in case of emergencies there were a couple of landline phones on hand.

Chapter Seventeen: They Tried To Make Me Go To Rehab

For many years I actually did say: 'No... no... no!' I was petrified of giving in to such a thing, because for me rehab seemed like the end of the road: a dead end of which there was no way of turning back. Anyway, years later and at the end of my tether I was coerced and convinced and there I was sat in the back of my manager's car on a road to ruin – or was it?

On the drive down I chatted with Lee; I knew how busy he was but was hoping he would have time to carry on writing the book, which during the call he assured me that he would, and he and I chatted for the entire journey. For the most part Lee is the consummate professional but at times when I need him, he's every bit as crazy as me. And during the drive down we joked about my whole sorry affair.

Lee poked fun at the idea of rehabilitation saying that he hoped he was wrong but to make sure I found out quickly which of the orderlies had their palms out ready for greasing. I was distraught at the idea of this, saying surely that wouldn't be the case. Was I wrong?

We also chatted about the future and what our plans where re the book etc when I was released. However, no sooner had we got into the conversation we'd arrived, and it was now time to say goodbye. "See you on the other side!" I joked as the wheels crunched their way through the gravel filled road in the lead up to the doors. "Yes, see you in a better place!" Lee replied as we said our goodbyes. "Good luck, sweetheart... here's to an improved you!" he said as the phone went down and I made my way into the Clouds.

I very quickly became institutionalised, which gave me a better understanding of Charlie and his incarceration. On my wall I had pictures of him and a board where I could put personal things messages etc. I had many wonderful roommates who over a short time became like sisters to me. Olivia, Kym, Charlie Bear, Emily, Shelly, Alyson to name just a few. I made so many friends in rehab all with a different story to tell. Rehab was a surreal experience and no sooner had I parked my butt in there did I end up being grassed up for taking painkillers. These were actually for my back pain, and the hypocrisy of it was that the girl who grassed me up was herself taking pills and storing for nobody to see. Anyway, as is always the way for me they fell for her story and they flushed my painkillers down the toilet. But anyway, who really gives a damn about rehab? Who actually supposes these places do a beneficial job? Well for starters I did!

I honestly believed that these places were run under the strictest of regimes. I thought these places were of the most brutal: like borstal for junkies - but oh, how wrong could a girl be? Well, I certainly was about Clouds House where Jane Moore and the team at Loose Women sent me. Oh yes, from the outside it certainly appeared aesthetically grand: a building fit for a king. However, behind those nineteenth century Wiltshire walls it was a sham. I'm confident that its architect Philip Webb, if ever to rise from the grave would be horrified to see what his extravagant pile of bricks and mortar had become. All I'm saying is this, in my humble opinion they should have left it as it was prior to 1983 and had done with it.

In my professional evaluation … pfft, this gaff was a bloody shambles, and its fully integrated round-the-clock hands on expert care was totally and utterly inadequate and nondescript! For all intents and purposes this supposed cloud of comfort for the broken, was nothing more than a posh-knobs den of iniquity. A place where overnight I became the house matriarch, as I played mother to a bunch of repeat offenders with ascending desire to be momentarily cured; A group of mentally failing men and women looking for a crutch to survive, and boy did we find it! Listen, even the orderlies could be bought, and for the price of a Costa Coffee and a word in the right ear, the three for a tenner selection of wines from the alcy's Willy Wonka aisle at Asda certainly did flow. As did, for a few dollars more, the illegal prescription Dr. Ugs from an earmarked, ready, and willing dealer at a nearby spieler. And again, in monotonous reiteration: 'Oh, what a farce.'

Colin drove my mum down one day in my car with the mirror hanging off. I told him to replace it and take it out of the rent, but I had no idea he wasn't paying any rent at all. Of course he told me he did, but it was all lies.

The hardest thing there was when I was thrust a paper from a male friend saying "Ere have look at that. It's your Charlie". It was full coverage of the Leeds trial re the attack on the governor at Wakefield. I had written to him while I was in there and he had written back saying he had a lot coming up, but reading the paper like that was horrific and it was in everyday, sometimes with photos of me, sometimes not. My friend Kym would get it quickly and take him out as I just couldn't handle it. I remember crying and just getting on with my jobs. We all had jobs it reminded me of what boarding school might be like.

Anyway, on a frantic Sunday just three and a half weeks into my stay I was kicked out. Nurses who had been lovely with me even turned against me. A councillor there tried desperately to help me, but it was no use; I was kicked out and, in the haste, I didn't even get the chance to say any proper goodbyes.Two hours later, while sat alone on one of two trains home, I ordered a large glass of Chardonnay and I didn't stop drinking until I got home. It was wholly unfair and the actions of a few, who clearly did not understand what had happened, threw me out. They were equally as cold when I picked up my belongings.

I told Colin if he was doing drugs to not to do them in front of me and it would be dangerous to have alcohol in the house and please don't have anyone in the house. I felt so strong but being thrown out in the way that I had been, I fell straight back into it and there was still no word from Charlie regarding the divorce.

Christmas came and we had a celebration for my mum's birthday in this lovely old pub all lit up for Christmas, but I couldn't handle all the people and the relatives looking at me. Was I drinking? Yes I was. It's the only way I thought I could handle the panic attacks. I had a major one and told Stoat and my brother and sister in law that I couldn't cope, I needed to go. "OK, we will take you home". "No, I mean go from this earth." I was incredibly suicidal, once again my dear friend Stoat came to the rescue.

Mark my manager took me back to Clouds House to collect my things and we had a long chat. He said when my phone was on it literally did not stop. Calls, emails, texts and messenger. He read some of them and replied saying who he was but what was apparent was just how many people who suffer from addiction and mental health problems turned to me for help and advice. Mark asked if I usually reply to any of these, I told him I reply to every one of them. "No wonder you are not well, you have to make time for yourself to heal" he said.

Charlie rang eventually, after I was out of rehab and we had a really long, good conversation. I was over the moon he got a not guilty for the incident in Wakefield. I was shocked (as was Charlie). It could've meant another ten years, of course the incident wasn't the violent affair the papers and media had made it out to be and the jury saw that, but his other violent offences at Frankland couldn't be so easily dismissed.

I was a little confused to what was happening now between me and Charlie. Letters were being sent again frequently and he sent me things to include in this book. Without prompting by me he wrote the foreword, things seemed to be improving. He had an art exhibition coming up and he asked me to be there for each day of the exhibition. It had all been arranged whilst I was inside rehab.

Before that though, I had an amazing holiday planned to Australia; a place I always wanted to visit. Stoat had two friends out there whose wedding he attended and photographed. It had been planned for 6 months. Stoat was worried that I would make a fool of him with my drinking but I assured him it wouldn't happen. We barely made the flight though as I was up cleaning until around 3am so decided to have a little sleep but woke up late. I had to throw all sorts in my case (90% of which I didn't use) and we raced there in my battered Nissan. Still, by skin of our teeth, we made the flight.

I really did need this holiday as things had been awful at home. Colin was lying to me a lot to get out of paying the rent. Also, on the Sunday I got kicked out of rehab he had promised to bring my mum down. She said if for any reason he couldn't make it that he could text or call her at any time, day or night. Yet he completely ignored her. Mum had given him petrol money (which I got back for her) and neighbours were reporting lots of comings and goings at my house. Colin said he was off drugs but God knows. My calls to him were always so nice but once back after the initial lovely greeting things weren't right and all my friends and family and Charlie were telling me to ask him to leave. I didn't trust a word he said and he would take three days to recover from his weekend out which meant him literally rotting on the sofa with those sodding housewife programmes on.

It had got to the stage I felt uncomfortable in my own home. His room was beyond a joke but that was his space and I never said a thing to him about it. I knew what he was doing, he was hanging on for as long as he could without paying rent until he had somewhere else to live. And then he went and picked a futile argument when he came home drunk and when he said he was leaving I was extremely chuffed. He was using my place with total disrespect, I would keep my mouth shut so much just to keep the peace, then I found out he been lying to me about the reason he couldn't pay the rent. He said his boss' dad was dead. She rang me at 10pm one night and asked what on earth has Colin said, so I told her and told her I was deeply sorry about her losing her dad, to which she replied that her dad had been ill but was okay and she had paid Colin every Friday. Furthermore, Colin had started to use my home for mobile clients and was cheekily using my car to ferry them about.

Looking back, I was mad to keep him so long but the last time I asked him to leave he said his parents wouldn't have him and he had nowhere to go and I'm a soft touch. Not these days though, I have learnt a lot and it took me a good while to clean that room. I'm surprised it wasn't infested. I was very upset at Colin. We had been friends since we were 12 years old at high school and I believe he was only staying with me as I had no kids, we had lot of female single friends but they had kids so I was the easy option. Plus I was rent free and a total mug but some days I hadn't the energy to move and to leave the house was so hard.

Colin then rang me and threatened to ruin me, some thanks for giving him a home eh? I told him he done it all to himself by lying so much. One time I had surgery in Manchester and he was meant to pick me up the following day but he got too trashed and came home later that day in such a state I had to call an ambulance and man-handle him, a 6ft man who was hanging off his bed crying about all-sorts. I was meant to be resting and he knew it, Stoat rescued me that day. So, leaving that day for Australia saw my dad move in and some debt collectors called looking for Colin, but apart from that Dad looked after the cats and house for me.

The people we stayed with, Vanessa and Penny, were a lovely couple. I was nervous as I didn't know them and I wasn't in the best mental state but their lovely ways and the sunshine and spending time with Stoat was really therapeutic, but I still felt a sense of isolation. They didn't know much about me and Charlie and nothing about my rehab episode and all I had been through. I didn't want them to know at all, I simply wanted to try and be free.

It quickly became apparent that my fitness was appalling and compared to their svelte figures, I honestly felt like a giant. All three of them were so lean and because of this I was very often found lagging behind. I had always had a smaller frame; I'd always had an hour-glass figure, only now I had a little more sand and because of this my usual brisk holiday walks had turned into a slow slump; the shock I had endured while away had taken its toll and I had really let myself go. To be honest, as much as it stuck in my craw, Charlie was right when he warned me to be careful about gaining weight, but when you feel depressed to the point of suicide the last thing you want to do is take yourself off to a bloody gym; a place where everyone struts their supposed high-octane mental state through ripping muscles that are desperately trying to break out of their sprayed on spandex t-shirts. Nope, sorry love ... the gym ain't no place for a girl like me ... I'll stick to a couple of baked bean cans and a makeshift wire flex skipping rope at home.

Charlie wanted some photographs, so I sent some to Rod and he kindly had them printed off for me and handed them to Charlie - I was so afraid of Charlie's reaction to them. I mean, I'd had a remarkable time travelling around Australia but I vowed that should I ever make the trek again I'd be a whole lot fitter, 'cos even though I was on other side of the world my anxiety in regard to my weight never left me. I would wake up early and wouldn't dare to leave the room frightened that I would have to make small talk with people.

My pet hate is when people ask: "Are you okay?" And I'd think to myself, well, would you like the real answer or the truth? You see, in Oz (Australia) I was very conscious of my drinking habits; I knew that if I drank heavily, I'd have to be careful to of what I said. And choosing not to speak about what had happened the last few years of my life meant that I couldn't truly be myself. I also hurt my foot over there which made it painful to climb over rocks and things, but I loved Australia and it is most definitely somewhere I will one day return to. I also have friends in Argentina and this is another country I try and visit every few years, but if I can't get out there, they visit me.

I have friends all across the globe and I'm blessed to say I get messages from all over the world. However, due to certain events, my circle of close friends I have had to reduce and today, as my trust has severely been tested, I really only allow a select few in. Furthermore, my faith in others has also diminished, which is sad because I always like to be there if people ever need me. Nevertheless. I am determined to hold close the friends I have today; I absolutely treasure them as I do my family, and certain friends who I love but who left my side due to concern are slowly flooding back into my inner circle.

Australia gave me the confidence to not wear makeup, I had my eyelash extensions done but that was it. I had my brows tattooed on but they were at the stage where the scabs come off, anyone who knows me knows I wore make up since I was twelve. Now though I'm trying to find some love for me for who I am. I'm worth loving, I'm a kind person and I adore animals and children and decent people.

I started to cut off from any gangster groups on Facebook but Charlie and I were still talking on the phone and writing to each other and I was trying to sort out accommodation with Beverleigh Zacher and Jules Preston, who I was going to share an apartment with for his upcoming art show. Really, in all honesty I could not afford the best part of a week in London, but I wanted to be there for Charlie. Then I got a phone call from Charlie "Oi you, don't you dare show up for my fackin' art exhibition". I was utterly perplexed wondering if he'd got the wrong number, "You've done fack all for me, and you don't deserve to show your face at my art show. Everyone will be there but I don't want you there, you're useless!"

Bronson was back, only this time he was on the end of long phone line and not behind bars in front of me. Nevertheless, at first my reaction was exactly the same as I couldn't talk: "Are you fackin' there? Cause your using up my precious time!" To which I abruptly replied, "I'm here ... how dare you say I've done nothing for you Charlie!" At which point he tried to butt in, but I forcefully continued, "You know what Charlie? That's absolutely fine, I will cancel all plans right this minute." As I promptly slammed down the receiver I contacted Bev and Jules and they both said they wouldn't be going, as they were mainly going to support me, and I believed them. You see, in the past, the two of these ladies have given Charlie a piece of their minds, it seemed we were the only people in the country who ever had the balls to stand up to the man; because no man ever did!

Daz called after and said that Charlie had agreed to divorce me. He also asked for Charlie's legal stuff (which I got ready and prepared for him) and the artwork he had given me. "No way!" I replied. "Tell your 'boss' I'm his wife and the art is mine: I know his ex, Lorraine had a load of his art, and Rod has many others, so why should I give mine back?" The art sent to me was mine and I was about to walk away from this with nothing, well I'm at least going to keep the artwork he gifted me.

Anyway, I got to see photos of everyone else at his art show. Cheers for that! Including his first wife Irene; it was nice to see her it was nice to see them all, but not a soul except for Rod had done anything in comparison to what I'd done for the man. It hurt me, it really did, but as ever I protected Charlie and the masses had no idea why I wasn't there.

A little while later after his visit with Charlie, Rod phoned to pass on an instruction. At which point I was trying to decorate my house as a ploy to distance myself from the whole affair; I was desperate to reprogram my brain after being hurt and betrayed by both Charlie, but even more, Colin. Rod informed me that Charlie wanted me to do an article in the paper regarding my refusal to visit him wearing a cat suit. Oh apparently, he was also annoyed that I had got him a ham and Coleman's mustard sandwich and had gone mental about the Coleman reference. Mind you, for some reason, after a little bit of deliberating I said I would think about the cat suit.

Incidentally, A past boyfriend who I mentioned briefly earlier had upset Charlie by slaughtering me publicly on social media; Charlie issued a subtle threat to him that leaked to the tabloids and Michael Coleman shat himself and sent Charlie a letter with a twenty quid note inside: like Charlie need's twenty notes the patronising git! Charlie didn't take very kindly to this gesture and slated the boy in the press saying: "You or anybody got anything to say - tell me when I'm out." And in closing Charlie added: "And I'll be out sooner than a lot think... Paula is my key, can't wait." Now that right there was enough to put the fear of god in most people and Coleman was no exception and according to mutual friends he lives in fear of the thought of Charlie's release. And that right there is a case of the bully being bullied.

Anyway, back to reality. So, Charlie rang me and asked me to get it in the paper, saying it would make him laugh; so, in it went, and my fee was a measly fifty quid. See with fees like these I'm sure you can see that it's definitely not the money I'm in it for. The article went online and was also featured in a small section of one the national rags (newspapers). So that was that, I had done the last silly story I was prepared to do, however, weeks later, much to my annoyance, Rod put a link to the story on his site and announced to Charlie's many followers that this was the kind of stupid story that did not help Charlie's cause one bit; for goodness sake, Charlie pleaded with me to do it! And then laughed about it incessantly.

Furthermore, there was a story, which I assumed Rod had done, with regards to Charlie complaining that HMP Woodhill (where he had now been sent) weren't serving up his fish and chips on a Friday anymore! Now, are you telling me that a story such as this ,that is an attack on the prison, wouldn't cause Charlie more damage? Pfft, c'mon lets have it right Rodney, of course it would. This story simply made him look like he was a moaning old git! Anyway, I retaliated by saying: "What everyone needs to understand about Charlie is that he courts the media. Moreover, if a certain person can't get a deal for a story Charlie will ask somebody else to try."

It was so annoying, 'cos, each time I was mentioned in any story I was either ridiculed or cruelly made fun of. Look, I have worked the comedy circuit including the Edinburgh Fringe, so I'm not afraid of a barrage of banter and can always laugh at myself, but these people who didn't know me, and have no right to pass vile judgements are always the first in the queue with the nasty comments. Why is this? Well Charlie always said that it was jealousy and fear of something that is different and they're envious of the fact that I'm strong enough to follow my heart.

Charlie had asked me if I could divorce him because he had a lot on. I looked into it and the simplest way was to get it annulled. I asked Charlie for the £550 to pay for it; this was the first time I had asked him for money and to his credit, he quickly had £600 transferred across to me and I was very pleased; you see, from one minute to the next you never could tell which Charlie you were going to get. Luckily enough, after looking into it and realising the cost, which I could ill-afford, Charlie stepped in and said he'd cover the cost; I obviously caught him on a good day.

My health, both mentally and physically had taken a bit of a downhill slide, and I kept waking up feeling as if I was unable to breathe, which resulted in me having a huge asthma attack, and yet again I was admitted to hospital with pneumonia. Charlie called me sounding concerned, but then quickly moved on to something else. I told him as soon as I got released from hospital, that I would sort out the annulment. He was happy with that and said: "Yes Paula, then somewhere down the line we can shock everyone again and get married for a second time." In a sense, I imagine that meant that this parting certainly wouldn't be the final goodbye. Perhaps Charlie underestimated my strength and sense of survival through it all.

The Sun newspaper ran a story about our marriage and its annulment, and immediately Rod posted it to his site! The paper called me up first, so I gave them a few comments in support of Charlie, but it was still obvious to me that Rod was having a pop at me on the site for speaking to them first. He also (I found out a month earlier) had the very person leading the hate campaign against me on the site he runs for Charlie and he's always been on there and that's how his information about me had been so accurate, which lead him to take to his own page and slag me off. Not once during any of the above did Rod ever stick up for me, and he knew more than anyone how much graft I had put into Charlie's cause, and also how much anguish these keyboard warrior's had put me through. Rod said: "Think of what Charlie has had to endure with what went on at Frankland?" To which I say, "Er, let's get it right, Charlie wouldn't have been sent to bloody Frankland if he hadn't have kicked off..." Thankfully, Charlie won the trial and I was extremely pleased for him.

The Governor of Wakefield, Mark Doherty was a complete twat, but if he'd have kept it together as he was meant to by allowing the legal team to deal with us and the debacle over our wedding photos, everything would've been ok. This was grossly unfair, especially when, to the prison's benefit, I would have done a whole host of positive media; in fact, everything to do with that had already been arranged. And if Charlie didn't want me to do something, I obviously wouldn't have done it. It was soul-destroying, I had put my entire reputation and career on the line for him and lost.

Once it was public knowledge that our marriage was going to be annulled, I began receiving loads of messages from men asking to take me out, "Thanks, but no thanks!" I said. "What, just so you can have a selfie with Bronson's bird? Well no, it ain't happening!" And then, almost immediately, I started to receive an overabundance of other requests too, some were rather rude, if you know what I mean? Oddly, an Arab who was apparently fascinated with me, wanted to fly me to Dubai and pay me well for my time. I think we all know where that was leading! Anyway, I politely declined. Then, there was a company in LA who wanted me to star in a porn film, and I was offered a considerable amount of money to do it. Nevertheless, (contrary to bullies' belief's) that's certainly not something I want to be getting involved in.
Charlie always wanted me to be a dominatrix, but I had to explain to him that it

wouldn't help his next parole hearing a great deal; his very own wife practising in dungeons, with methods of torture waiting at home for him on his release. To be honest, and due I'm sure to his many years spent incarcerated, quite often Charlie sometimes fails to see the bigger picture. Such as the brain-wave they had to produce fitness protein powder that he would endorse. After reading that particular story I quite literally and emphatically said, "Oh Charlie ya' daft sod, to endorse a product you have to take it. Just sticking your mug on it whilst you're in prison ain't going to sell it." And I was right, 'cos it was an epic fail; so that was a nice little '36 bags' flushed down the carsi. Charlie called me to tell me, but without rubbing salt into already sore wounds, I tried to delicately explain that it was ridiculous idea from the start. Charlie changed the subject rather quickly at this point. Like many men, he had a hard time agreeing that he was wrong. Furthermore, it also contradicts the idea of solitary fitness, which, for the record, is a fantastic idea.

Moving onto something a little more realistic, I had promised Charlie everything, and was determined to see it through; we had even discussed where we would live and had even looked at properties on various real-estate websites. I had got him a brilliant manager and agent and things were in progress for him to have a comeback fight, for charity. If it could have been done then it would have been done. We would have lots of security and I would have very gently re-introduced him to the world he would have had on civvy street, with his own art studio and an unlimited source of supplies. Moreover, I would have protected him and made sure his dreams all came true, and of that he had my word. However, in his ultimate wisdom, and due, on my behalf to a momentary lack of good judgement, he chose to let me go.

Charlie has his own reason for the split, and they weren't simply down to that one stupid photo taken with a group of gay lads. Charlie sometimes asks the impossible of people, not realising how long things take in the real world to organise; Charlie places a lot of demand on those closest to him. For a case in point, take his manager and friend, Rod. Now Rod is in his 70s, and works like a pack horse for Charlie's cause, and I fear that it may be the death of the poor man. I mean look at me, I was frequently ill from the things he had me running around doing, yet at that time I kept most of it under wraps.

I honestly believe (in fact, I know) that if it wasn't for all of Charlie's yes men, and if he was just a prisoner like the rest of the herd, he would be doing everything to make our marriage work, because as he so rightly said on numerous occasions: "With you swee'art, I dare to dream of a future!" Which was similar to what Charlie had spoken at length with Ronnie Kray about in Broadmoor. Ron's dream was to be out on civvy street, living with his twin brother, Reg, in Suffolk, and almost in parallel to this, Charlie and I wanted a cottage, and let me tell you this, it wasn't just a silly pipedream. I had a lot of dealings with Charlie via a legal perspective and it's not as foolish as some would imagine.

Nevertheless, at present, Charlie is happy where he is. Only the other day did I receive a letter from him telling me that he had just finished his time on the yard and then done his workout on the multi gym, which was finished off with a relaxing soak in the bath, then back to his cell for dinner and to watch some TV and do a bit of his highly celebrated and much-loved artwork. Then, he would have a read of a book, look at a few letters, then it would be back for more TV and food, followed by a few more exercises before going to bed where, in his words: "I sleep like a baby…" And yes, I bet he bloody does – it ain't a bad life, now is it?

People have always thought that I was in it for what I could get, and it simply was never the case. Listen, I have so many things such as that letter that I could sell for bundles, people just don't know the half of it. My name and my reputation has suffered immensely from me being used as some cash-cow scapegoat. Well, at this point in my life I'm quite happy to say, no more! These days I will do what is necessary for me and the betterment of my life and the people I hold dearest, which right now includes, drafting out this book with my writer friend, Lee; a book that will, once and for all, reveal the full irrefutable story.

But will there ever be life after Charlie? Well of course there will, I just need to get my brain in gear and move on. I live in hope of one day divorcing my dependency on the mixed-up remedies that I concoct for myself; the remedies that I use to heal my mental state of mind. I mean, I wasn't born this way: I didn't exit my mother's womb tarnished and tainted and needing a crutch, it was obviously something that etched its way under my skin and somehow found its way into my DNA. It appears to be a part of me now, and for all intents and purposes I believe I am destined to live life on the edge of sanity with paradise on the other side of the fence: mockingly stirring back at me, and that right there is nobody's fault, for the frail state of mental well-being I was feeling from a very young age seemed to have been written in the stars for me.

My parents never really knew the extent of my problems… whose parents do? Listen, whose parents are ever entirely privy to the ups and downs of their children's lives and, for that matter, whose parents would ever want to be? It's just not the way life goes!

Chapter Eighteen: A Lorry load of Dreams

I pleaded with my fractured nervous system to let me be … and with hands clasped tight, I prayed at the foot of my bed to the big man one night: "Please Lord, send me a soul-mate…" And with breath baited my prayer was answered, as a knight on his trusty steed gallantly thundered towards me. Oh OK, sod the 'Mills and Boon' guff, so it was a man called Peter Jones (not off the Den of Dragons fame) in a big bloody shiny XPO diesel truck - but hey, I'm sure you get the picture? Anyway, whatever the scene, he was my shining knight all the same.

Pete entered my life, and for the most part put me back on the straight and narrow, and for the time I spent under his guidance, death and all its devastation had been securely locked away in a drawer along with my many dark thoughts of impermanence. Nevertheless, I knew, right there in that moment that the drawer was only temporarily locked, and unfortunately one day, if the mood overtook me, I could recall those death inducing digits in a heartbeat and unlock the demons, and to be quite honest that day was never far from my mind. However, for that day, and for as far as I could see over the horizon, I was safe: safe from the destiny my frail infrastructure had menacingly mapped out for me. Pete was my sanctuary; a giant buoy for me to cling to if the waters got too choppy, and this I did on many occasions.

Anyway, while finishing decorating and de-cluttering my house this week I spoke to Charlie, and I'll be divorcing him imminently. I wanted to keep this hush hush for a time, for our ears only! And only the inner sanctum of the inner circle shall know. I then rung Lee my good friend, who incidentally happens to be my co-writer. I wanted his advice in regard to where we go next with the manuscript. To Lee I guess, it always seems as if I'm procrastinating, but I'm not, it's simply me and the war I have with anxiety; if the house isn't clean it plays havoc with my mental well-being which has a damaging effect on my concentration. I need to clear the place of rubbish and create an ambience of inspiration; because hopefully, it's here, in this dwelling, where I will write something truly special – well that is at least the hope.

I was telling Lee that Pete had recently started finishing (oxymoron alert) off the decorating at home and doing a deep de-clutter in the week. It had to be done as it was driving me insane! I also told him that I had spoken to Charlie and that it was now truly over and this was something I hoped to keep under my hat for a short while, not that Charlie would do the same, 'cos he was probably already onto his next 'promotional vehicle'. I told Pete that I would only be informing my closest friends and no one else at that time, simply because once the 'paps' got a hold of it, I'd be fair game for the next few weeks of saucy headlines. Oh, and re the house clean. I quickly rang Lee first and told him the news, I only told Lee in case he thought I was procrastinating – AGAIN! I'm not in the habit of boring my male friends senseless with menial crap. Nevertheless,

Lee's a good egg, a dear friend and has been right by my side through this whole ridiculous farce – and 'Oh, what a farce,' it had been.

During this time Lee had setup a meet with his literary agent to discuss my story; my manager wasn't altogether happy about the meet because he knew that this little liaison would have nothing whatsoever to do with him and his money grabbing company. Mark you were a top manager, and for a time a good friend, so this I say very lightly, I'm so sorry, but in some ways, you were like the rest. Part of the fibres on a tightening noose around my neck.

The proposal, submission or whatever it is that Lee call's it, I believe is complete. I sent over my extensive notes and Lee (the clever sod) magically re-wrote them. Now, I'm not one to blow smoke up someone's arse, but when credit is due I am the first to vocalise it, and such an accolade I will be vocalising to Lee, for the work he has done has had my emotions on high alert; not least the work he has done on the section about my Grandparents which is truly remarkable: so touching in fact, it immediately brought on the waterworks. Bloody hell, I know I've poured my heart out to him, but to what extent I was simply unaware.

So, that's everything in hand, the proposal, mine and Lee's brief profiling bio's and a tastefully chosen selection of photographs depicting the stages of my life all in a folder and ready for a trip down The Smoke (London). Pete 'my trusty knight' is driving me - I do hope he's remembered how long I can chat. But Pete is a darling, and not one to complain. To be honest, I think he's sent from the film noir age, 'cos believe me, his morals and values certainly do echo back to a bygone age.
'We're off, we're off, we're off in a motorcar, sixties cops are after us…'
Talk about echoing back to a different time and place, as we typed those lyrics that shot to the forefront of my mind, I was on a coach all mini skirt and pony tails, heading up the motorway on a school trip with egg sarnies and monster munch; but cease my wandering mind and let's get back to the trip in hand.

Pete has the car running and after my fifteenth nervous toilet stop, and we were finally on the move. I've called Lee and he's telling me that he hope's I'm wearing something a little risqué? Risqué enough, he says so as to set his book agent's heart a flutter. Lee knows me only too well, he knows how well equipped I am at using what God gave me to get the job done – this girls been there, done it, well let's face it, I invented the bloody t-shirts. Many would see this act of over the top extrovertedness (if that's even a word) as somewhat sluttish! But it isn't at all, a singer sings a few bars, a footballer kicks a few tricks, and I simply show 'em what I've got, and in this case, it just 'appens to be my ample bosom! Anyway, who cares, the haters would hate me even if I lived in a shagging nunnery!

Chapter Nineteen: A Public Flogging

I never set out to upset anyone! My objective in life has always been to do the exact opposite. What is it with me, well some say these faceless keyboard clickers are simply jealous? Now, girls with such a gripe I can sort of understand, for some reason a certain echelon of females have always loathed and detested me, but men with a similar hang up I find a bitter pill to swallow. So, were these deep-seated feelings that overwhelmed a certain array of people really due to my union with one of the world's most infamous, and dare I say dangerous prisoners, 'cos if I'm honest, to me that sounds like something of a scapegoat; a vehicle for these people to set sail their incomprehensible hatred. Nevertheless, for a time, the wind from those savage sails almost took my breath away.

Those couple of years from 2017-2019 brought about some of the most difficult times of my life: for the most part my family had kicked me and my feelings to the curb, although in part, I understood their concerns, but, at such a troubled and prickly time I could have honestly done with their backing. I mean, Mum and Dad are old-school which I guess is a polite and new age way of saying antiquated. But my brothers, well that's a different story, I really hoped at least they would have ridden the crest of the proverbial wave in support of me. So, will there ever truly be a life after this man? For one thing we're both adults, and he and I said we will remain friends no matter what. Of course, Charlie's mum and I will stay in touch, not only because we share the same friends and acquaintances, but also because we struck up a mother in-law, daughter bond. So, I will always do my best if ever I'm needed. What is more important is that I need to learn to put my life back together; I have many goals and many avenues I still wish to pursue.

Oddly enough I'm fascinated with the idea of becoming a mortician, this may simply be because I require a certain amount of peace and quiet in my life! Additionally, I would also take it as an honour to make a family's loved one at the end of their days look their ultimate best. But above all I plan to work with various charities. I want BPD (Bipolar Disorder) and other personality disorders to be spoken about openly, in order for people to understand it – because 'it' is a very complex disability. Due to my BPD, I have filtered my circle of friends down to a very small and select group. There are times when I feel like I'm slipping away, and it's damned hard work living in my mind. So, all the bullies out there needn't have bothered berating me, I give myself a far harder time than they ever could. But hear this, one thing that is unwavering is my will to survive … I simply refuse to be beat. And with every single knockdown I get up twice as strong!

This brings me to a brace of my lifelong heroines, Anne Frank and Madonna, slightly different anomalies I know, but that's my crazy ass brain for you. Anne was a wonderfully intelligent young lady, who would've gone on to achieve amazing things had she not, along with her sister Margot, after being spared immediate death in the Auschwitz gas chambers, instead being sent to Bergen-Belsen, a concentration camp in northern Germany. In February 1945, the Frank sisters died of typhus at Bergen-Belsen, and their bodies were thrown into a mass grave; only a week later came liberation. To me, Anne is a person to truly look up to. She would always see the good in people despite living in such a horrendously, troubled time. Hitler on the other hand, as all cowards finally do, retreated to his hole and gave up. I'm wondering, as you no doubt are, why I'm talking about Anne Frank. But why not, she was and is a great symbol of hope strength and positivity. I have visited the Anne Frank House or her 'Secret Annexe' in Amsterdam many times and it never fails to move me.

Madonna, I guess, is a hugely different entity, but is she? Madonna has worked tirelessly for all she has in this world, and even to this day dares to use her status and power in the music industry to stand up and be counted. Madonna is a political force, she is a mother, she's also a global super star, an artist, and someone who I will forever admire. She is my queen and I will endeavour to follow her as she tours her brilliance around the globe. I'm inspired by many people and this, I now see as the next chapter in my life; I mean let's face it, the last bloody one was huge.

I came up against a nation who judged me and condemned me, and I hope this book has dispelled some of the myths and laid out my journey for what it was … the simple truth. Charlie also inspired me to be strong and to do what you have to do, and to this day, the man still does. Our connection will never be broken as we will always be in close contact. But for now, I have to pick up the pieces of a broken life and put them back together, get my life back, as firm as bloody cement, and build it once again.

There are days when I can't bear to even be seen, and on certain days my inner voice … the one that refuses to let my heartbeat just won't let up. And, although there is actually no reason why I should still be alive, this is the voice I allow to guide me – for I blindly follow no one. I predict that a vast number of things will happen with Charlie, and to be honest, one thing is for sure, I know he still has at least one more prison marriage in him. I also know that he's doing well, and that pleases me so much. However, the moment it starts not heading the way he has planned it in his bonce, he will certainly make his distain known, in whatever way he sees fit. I obviously know Charlie will read this book, and I hope he gives me credit for being honest, open, and ultimately fair. I hope he completes his time in incarceration and then finally gets to walk out of those prison gates and feels the sun on his face a free man.

Also, I hope he gets to enjoy the 'happy ever after' ending he so longs for; I just know it will not be with me. To Charlie's supporters, thank you but do not simply be blinkered and blinded by the man's notoriety, do not be pushed around, for you have your own lives to fulfil outside those prison walls. And for goodness sake, do not follow his lead, make use of the vast array of work programmes, do all the training you can and until that day comes when you walk out of those iron gates. Make that prison time work in your favour.

Having a strong opinion of someone is one thing, but publicly ridiculing them to a baying audience of thousands is shameful - isn't it? I am right in that assumption - yes? I do hope the answer to that queues up a resounding and deafening scream of - YES!

Berated, humiliated, taunted, butchered, are there anymore verbs you'd like to add? By God they fought hard to ostracize me. But for what reason? Why would any individual member of a group whose administrators remit, that was widely broadcasted to (as gangsters do) look after their own, so provokingly hang me out to dry? Well let's lay it out for all to see:

Right, so I'm a failing actress who courted the press while entering into a relationship with the country's most dangerous prison inmate? Please use the blank piece of paper provided to jot down your answers. Oh, there isn't one, it was proposed, but the publisher thought it was a ridiculous idea, and it was! But please don't rush off and start a group, mustering up an army of followers, in 'daft ideas' retaliation.

So, let me very quickly dissect the above proclamation: as to the first point, I wasn't a failing actress. I was on the rise, my agent had an array of work coming in for me and I was due to leave for America in the months following my hook up with Charlie. However, due to my hook-up with Charlie I was professionally kicked to the curb; not a soul would hire me ... so much for the leg up to stardom, it almost destroyed me, and my acting career was in tatters! It was an abomination. And many times, I asked myself: 'Why Paula, why do you have to always go with your heart and your emotions?' Especially when, as has many times been proven, you've ended up losing everything you've ever worked for! But it's just the way I am ... the way I'm built; I have never had the will to go into battle with my feelings because my feelings forever prevail. Furthermore, on most occasions much to the detriment of myself. So, where did it all start?

Well, it all began with an administrator from the Facebook group I mentioned earlier. This man seemed obsessed with me as he continued his on-slaught, purporting with a misplaced passion his negative opinion in regard to my hook-up with Charlie, and the damning effect it could have on the incarcerated man's progression. It was relentless, I honestly could not believe that one person could be so obsessed. I mean, he'd almost dedicated a whole bloody gangland site to naming and shaming said subject's wife to be. This man wasn't (as he has documented widely) and isn't the biggest fan of Charlie anyway: so, for him to bullyingly berate me publicly for the work I was being questioned about by the tabloids was ludicrous ... I mean, this man had set sail a ship of hatred, inserted (xx) Gordon Avenue, Sneyd Green into its chronometer and let a vast array of pirates, board it and immediately aid and abet his futile attack on me.

To be honest at first it was laughable, not a soul took it seriously and believed it would simply fade. I chatted extensively with my closest friends about it and the consensus was the same: they go back into their corners once they've got it out of their silly little systems. However, that wasn't to be; their berating, re Paula hating, escalated like a rocket heading for the stars, and as the effects of it began hitting me hard so did my abuse for fine wines. (OK, three for a tenner from Asda!) Anyway, 'to ease the pain' I used the plonk to swill down a daily increasing amount of prescription barbs (barbiturates.) Oh yeh, I told everybody that it wasn't bothering me, but hey, these are my beautiful friends and they knew only too well that it was steadily taking a vice-like hold on me.

At first, I really didn't see it as bullying, and I for one would not have placed myself in a group that housed the bullied. But I was wrong, as I was publicly flogged right there in front of anybody that chose to be a part of it. Men, women and even ex-boyfriends jumped on the bandwagon and fed the flames as they licked ever higher; it was appalling, brazen, and damn right, reprehensible.

So, to detail the aforesaid a little. Yes, that is correct, an ex-boyfriend joined the haters: I honestly never saw it coming, and in some way my shock is proof that we ended our relationship amicably. Nevertheless, he must have been deeply hurt by our split because the barrage of viciousness that speedily left his fingertips would have left a premier league keyboard warrior's digits wriggling in the dust. Yes, this man's mission to ruin me seemed to be his reason for living, and nothing or no one could stop him. I guess it was his unique way of self-harming: instead of cutting himself to relieve his pent-up tension, it would appear that throwing cheap, incomprehensible jibes my way was all the release he needed. Now, due to my selfless personality I feel any prospective admirers out there need to know what this man has to offer. Well for one thing this boy was loaded (he was in the driving seat of mummy and daddy's gravy train)! But anyway, he was in the money and bought fine cars aplenty to ease any distress brought on by his less than ample carnal apparatus. But hey, that's quite enough lip-service paid to the boy who said too much; the boy who still lives life while dangling from mummy's apron strings, the feckless supposed rave scene 'author' who used daddy's hard-earned gravy to flaunt his penchant for awful creative writing. So, let's move on from the aider and abetter who fuelled the repugnant public flogging. The Chinese whispers that were tossed back and forth over a net of snapping and snarling barrater's became Roy Castle trumpeting sized record breakers, and to be honest the rhetoric became so much a part of the social media fabric that even I started to bloody believe it.

Throughout the onslaught of abuse, I felt I was fading fast and I was clinging on by my teeth. The cruelty at the hands of a selection of trolling bullies was coming in thick and fast and I wasn't coping with it too well. Oh yes, to the outsider I put on a brave face but inside it was doing me in, and because of this I stepped up the cocktails a bit; I (without Pete knowing) ordered more 'prescription' drugs from eBay and tried to get through the day.

Most of my close friends knew what was going on and stepped up their comforting, somewhat. However, as soon as the doors closed at night and I was alone (as Pete was on long shifts) I just sat wallowing in the pain: foolishly reading the shit that was written about me, and because of this I quickly became grief stricken, falling into deep anxiety. And the only way I could get through the stress was to ramp up my intake of drugs and wine to wash it down. I was getting tired and simply couldn't deal with everything on my own.

I just feel so drained and so very low. I keep thinking I'll be okay, then suddenly I'm lower than before. I've been an addict for years and I finally need to address it or Charlie's right … I will be dead, and that's a fact! But sometimes I think that would be the better option, but I have to think of others. I've got funeral plans all in place; it's paid for, and all taken care of because I don't want to cause my poor parents any more trouble than I already have. I hope to god I can get through everything, but I'll be honest, sometimes I'm so tired and feel I've had enough, but then other times I feel I can fight… only time will tell. But whatever happens, thank you for absolutely everything you've done for me and for your unwavering friendship.

Chapter Twenty: Too Late For Goodbyes'

'Marilyn, Amy and Anna Nicole, please save me a seat,
'cos ladies, this girl is on her bloody way…'

This is the unfortunate part where I have to step in from the shadows and take over in the first person, not only as a writer, but as Paula's friend. And the reason for this, is my beautiful friend Paula slipped away with the world and wolves at her feet; lost in a darkness of which only she held the key. With hindsight, my discrete offers of support seemed somewhat fruitless; a beckoning that lacked strength to power her will and bring her back from a tyrannical brink. In her last few weeks Paula was contented… not entirely happy, just satisfied with the status quo she had found herself in. However, in Paula's head, it just wasn't enough, so she fuelled her fractured mental state with unearthly tonics! An overabundance of potions that would ease her pain for a time and mask out whatever it was that was fronting a blitzkrieg attack on her frail and descending mind.

One of the last questions Paula asked me: "Lee, you have your own Guardian Angels, don't you? Because I obviously have mine." But to my dismay I had no time to reply. However, in light of the events of July 29th, 2019, my answer is simply this, "My dearest friend Paula, I certainly have my guardian angel today!"

During the three weeks in the lead up to her death, over numerous voice notes and phone calls, Paula obsessed to me and her closest friends relentlessly about death. Because for some reason, along with the gutter-dogs on social media, the grim reaper seemed to be trolling her. This obstinate stalker was hot on her tail, and by 'eck did she know it! Paula spoke openly about her life and its impermanence, with words that were very matter of fact. However, the shake and quiver as the words fell from her lips made it unmistakably apparent that she was in fact petrified. Not afraid of the thought of dying. Oh no, just the thought of putting her mum and her new-found soul mate Pete through such an ordeal; an ordeal of such magnitude, that Mum, in her senior years could find a tide too strong to swim through.

However, as I have learned recently, through extensive chats with Hazel, this lady is old school and is well equipped mentally to compartmentalize her torturous thoughts and save them for another day … the day she meets her sweet loving daughter again. Now, Pete on the other hand is a different being, for Pete had found his one true love; a woman he loved from the very first moment their eyes met; a beautiful and unique lifeforce, that slotted right into his life like egg to his bacon, or, more poetically, a lady that held the key to his heart and his hers, as my recorded voice-notes clarify in testimony.

Just a handful of hours before her inevitable demise, on Saturday the 27th of July at eleven in the evening, a slightly inebriated Paula ordered her fiancée Peter Jones to fetch her a box of dressing up goodies and from it she produced a white wig, an evening dress, and a pair of elbow length opera gloves. And while playfully sipping from a white wine filled glass, she instructed her friend Nick Morgan (which was no easy feat) to interview her as she mirrored her idol, the originator of girl power, Madonna.

Paula was every inch the star, as she teased her cinematographer Pete on his less than adequate technique. But behind the gaiety it was very easy to see the struggle she was in; it was clear to see the failing interior hidden behind a veil; a veil she often wore to keep the wolf from the door. Paula's struggle for stardom hurt, and deep down it was killing her. In later years Paula courted gangster fame as a leg up into the world of celebrity. Paula's acting prowess was considerable, and it was a travesty that only a select number of eyes had the pleasure of witnessing it. Paula was the epitome of a method actor unearthed, a fact of which plagued her from the very first moment she donned that blonde wig and sang for her Gran, to the very last moment she ever sported it.

Well, the Saturday evening came and went and as Sunday was unfolding it was quite obvious to Pete that Paula wasn't well, but Paula always had bouts of mild illness, so it was nothing new. Paula suffered from IBS (Irritable Bowel Syndrome) and COPD (Chronic Obstructive Pulmonary Disease) and these together often, and quite understandably, knocked her off her feet a little. Anyway, Paula and Pete were up and about and Pete (Cinders) as Paula referred to him was doing his usual Sunday chores.

Paula's friend Nick was up from Cardiff and was staying over for the weekend, and they had arranged a night out before his trip back home. As the day went by, according to Pete, Paula was getting progressively worse and was being sick into a bucket as a result. Pete implored Paula not to go out and said that instead, he would go out later and get them some drinks and food and they could have a relaxing night in, thus giving her the chance to nurse her unwell state. Nevertheless, Paula was a pleaser, and because Nick was so desperate to go out on the town, she dutifully submitted, in the hope of somehow shaking off the illness as the evening progressed.

When the evening was upon them, they all left the house, leaving Pete tidying the house after their pre hitting-the-town drinks and making the house once again presentable for the rabbles return. During the evening Paula phoned and text Pete saying that she wasn't going to stay out too long because she was feeling increasingly worse. Pete took this as read and got himself ready to go out and fetch enough food for a last supper, which would be aptly befitting, given the events that, unbeknown to them, were about to transpire.

Pete kept running round his mind thinking of things Paula had been saying to him all day, morbid things like: "If anything happens to me… and If I don't come home…" Earlier that day while lying on the bed as Pete stroked her hair and kissed her, Paula was saying: "You'll find someone else to love …

There will be someone else for you to kiss." In hindsight, this all seemed like an unintended goodbye. And taking this into consideration and listening to many voice notes it seemed as though Paula was having a gut feeling that the end of her life was in sight and was delicately saying her goodbyes. And as Paula's absence increased, Pete grew more and more apprehensive.

According to reports from close friends Stoat, one of her closest friends, had offered to run her home early on into the night. Paula declined and Stoat left alone, apparently a little concerned for her wellbeing. Once Stoat was gone Paula sought out a dealer and bought herself some bags of coke (Cocaine); Pete later realised that she had transferred money from Pete's account, presumably to purchase what she needed. Pete flags this up as a point of interest because as he has stated: as a precaution he had only given her enough money for drinks, food, and taxis.

Soon after, and while Pete was waiting for her to return, they arrived home; Paula was worse for wear, ranting about some doorman (bouncer) who had refused her and her friends entry into a particular club … she was livid. And in her drunken state she proceeded to jump in her car and tried starting the engine, she was going off her head saying she was going to "Sort the bouncer out!" She was brandishing a bread knife for all the street to see, she was clearly overtaken and fuelled by drink and drugs. Pete managed to calm her down; appeasing her, saying: "Listen swee'art, come back in the house and I'll have a chat with the bouncer in question!" This worked and she did as Pete had asked. Pete had no intention of accosting said bouncer, he was simply going to park around the corner in the hope of this pacifying her – it worked.

Anyway, they all went back into the house, Pete (to calm her) poured Paula a small glass of wine and got Nick a can of cider from the fridge, then they left her in the room and went for a cigarette. In the mean-time, unbeknown to them Paula had snuck out of the house, taken the car and gone after the bouncer with the bread knife. Pete and Nick finished their cigarettes and went back in and quickly realised that Paula wasn't there when suddenly lights from a vehicle appeared on the drive, in front of the house; Pete was fraught, knowing exactly where she had been. Again, Pete managed to reason with her, and she eventually came into the house and went up to bed.

At this point Pete had a plan: he thought, it's three in the morning, I'll sleep downstairs and then I'll hear her if she ventures down and wants to go on the rampage again. He checked in on her and said she was (as anyone drunk would be) sprawled out on their bed and appeared to be in a deep sleep. Pete was happy and prayed she stayed in that position until morning; until daylight broke and the intoxicated, mad-crazed entity had left her. Also, Pete thought, Nick is in the other bedroom and might hear her if she moves as well. Pete went downstairs and tucked himself up on the sofa and tried to relax for a little shut-eye; only half-asleep mind, 'cos he wanted to be on high alert in case she made a move: she didn't, and unbeknown to Pete, unfortunately, she never would.

At around 6.30am Pete opened his eyes, and seeing the sunlight peeking through the curtains thought, *thank you, now I can go up and lay with her and completely relax.* He was wrong, because as he ventured upstairs and entered the bedroom, he immediately noticed that something was dreadfully wrong; Paula was spread-eagled: lifeless. She was gone! Pete tried to wake her, kissing her, pleading with her to wake, but it wasn't to be. He speedily left the bedroom and rang an ambulance. The paramedics arrived but were too late: Paula had passed, and Pete's life was about to take the most terrible of turns.

So, the time came, and at Paula's request the steed powered carriage with its pink plumes was drawn; solemnly making its way through the Stoke-on-Trent streets as Paula's final excursion was underway. A wealth of mourners (with cat treats in hand) strode delicately through the pathways of Paula's childhood memories. And in haste to get to the church on time, in full fab four Abbey Road style, Paula's sisters from other misters, stopped the traffic and took to the Zebra crossing, and with the passing of their sweet Northern Sister 'The Sheatles' were born.

These girls had been through the ringer with Paula and had stayed loyal and true throughout. A name that screams out from the pack is Beverleigh Zacher; Bev had fought the good fight with all her might against the trolls and the bullies; thus, putting herself and her stalwart reputation in harm's way, and all in defence of the lady she referred to as Queen P! Queen being a most befitting moniker for anybody who had the pleasure of her friendship.

The events of Paula's funeral are private and not something I'd choose to detail in length. However, what I will say is that it went off with a Queen P bang, and while a swarm of tabloid 'paps' laid in wait to unleash the first morsels of a story, the eulogies by close friends and family conjured up images of a much-loved girl with the weight of anxiety and all its hellish demons hot on her tail. Paula's life was celebrated just as she would have wanted, with colourful characters from up and down the UK regaling stories and anecdotes which highlighted a unique lady; a one-off woman that we simply don't see very often.

Yet even as I type, the stories of her life still creep around the minds of many, and with the inquest detailing the whys and wherefores of her passing still to be heard in September of this year 2020, the jury is still out regarding whether or not her death was accidental or an unrelenting necessity. But with resounding reassurance I am here to tell you this: Paula was taken from us early as a result of her addiction to prescription drugs; for when the mind is too powerful for a person's will to survive, the need for a crutch takes over. And according to many voice-notes and recorded phone calls, Paula had been fighting for her life for some time! Moreover, her fight had become something of a daily battle. And as the wine 'to ease her nerves' flowed, so did the popping of pills as a need to ease her through each day.

At this point in Paula's story, one thing I would like to say to Hazel is this: Hazel, please be thankful for the 38 years you had with your beautifully unique daughter, because unfortunately, from the very first day she started to question her own mortality at the impressionable age of 21, every subsequent year you had her in your life was a bonus.

And as Paula's mum Hazel has permitted me to convey: if Paula's life had turned a corner, and she had met her soulmate Pete a little sooner, her precious daughter Paula may still be with us today retelling her own ruinous, albeit philanthropic story. For Paula lived her life for others, the fact of which was bound to bite her on the ass one day. Anyway, as always, our Paula must have the final say, so I'll let her finish with a phrase I'm sure at this moment is urging its way from her many friends and family's lips:

"Oh, what a farce!"

Dedication by Peter Jones (in his own words and unedited)

My Perfect Princess, Paula By Peter Jones (Paula's Fiancé)

Paula is my life, my world, my everything my perfect dream woman and I am so very, very, much in love with her she will always be precious and perfect to me, Paula was so loving, caring and attentive. That was the real Paula, she would do anything to help anyone.

No one will ever know just what losing Paula has done to me mentally and physically. My heart and soul belongs to Paula and when Paula passed away, she took my heart and soul with her. I have never been allowed to grieve because all the judgemental and haters out there have made it impossible. I have had threats, I have been spat on. So many people turned their backs on me and stopped talking to me. I used to be so outgoing and bubbly now I find I can't even go through the door. I only go out when I think there is not many people about, I get so anxious at the thought of people seeing me as I don't need or want confrontation or to have to explain my relationship with Paula. I don't see anyone else having to explain their relationships, but the difference is I can prove my relationship with Paula but all the haters and judges out there don't want that happening as it will prove they didn't really know Paula and her life and it will prove that the mouthpieces were lying about me and God forbid they would have to apologise and be proved that they were lying.

I found myself going up against haters and defending myself and Paula and funnily enough so many against me were the same ones who were against Paula but now they were making out they were her friend and knew everything about her and spreading lies and making up stories about me, just like they did with Paula. Why can't they just accept the fact two people met and fell so deeply in love. It was like Paula was never allowed to move forward with her life but yet 3 days before she passed away Charlie actually announced he was getting married again once the annulment came through and you're not telling me that none of Charlies supporters didn't know, but did he get any grief? No he didn't, nor did the woman he was marrying getting any. He was allowed to move on, and why not? Everyone is entitled to be happy, so why was it so different for Paula? Because she had nothing but grief and bullying, but I must say Charlie never did give her grief. He only ever wished her well and always wanted her to be happy in life and find someone who she was happy with.

So what gave his supporters the right to bully Paula and stop her from moving forward? Paula was so frightened to tell anyone about us and that hurt her because she wanted to tell all her friends how happy she was and wanted a normal life but was never allowed. This caused so much depression and anxiety for Paula. So many people turned their back on me and stopped talking to me because of all the lies that were said about me. It doesn't matter how old you are or how strong you think you are. If you getting called all sorts of vile names and publicly humiliated and sent vile cruel messages all day, every single day it will damage you and if you're suffering with mental health problems too it definitely doesn't help you. Let me ask all you bullies who think its clever and hard and okay to set out to destroy someone how would you feel if it was your partner?? I guarantee you wouldn't like it, especially seeing your partner break down every day and wondering what they'd done to deserve all this. Ask yourselves that question before you attack anyone else.

Losing Paula absolutely destroyed me, I lost my whole world my life and my dream woman. We had so much planned and so much to look forward to in life. I am so devastated. Now my world and my soul are very empty and it's very lonely. I have nothing to look forward to. Actually, the only thing I have to look forward too is when I draw my last breath because when that day comes that will be the day I will be reunited with Paula. My heart is broken beyond repair.

I talk to Paula every day and listen and read her messages every day. I'm only existing until I can be back with Paula and this time no one can hurt us. There is only a few that knew about me and Paula and knew how we both felt about each other. To those few, I thank you so much for not following the pack of haters. I will never find the love and happiness I had with Paula. What we had together was absolutely amazing and perfect, I wish with all my heart everyone could have seen what we had together and how Paula felt about me and how I felt about Paula. I am so broken inside I can't even explain, I cry every day, and I am not ashamed to admit it. I'm so in love with Paula every day and wake up broken hearted and missing Paula so, so, much and pray every day that today is my last day here and I can be back with Paula for eternity.

I think of Paula every minute of every day, and even though the haters and liars have turned everyone against me and taken my life away from me just like they did with Paula with their vile hatred and lies, they will never ever take the happy and lovely memories of the love we have for each other the plans we had together and how happy we were together. These I will treasure until my last dying breath.

Life after Paula? To me there is no life after her because Paula was my life, my world and my everything. My heart was broken, and I knew it would never repair because my heart and soul belong to Paula always. There was never a cloudy day with Paula around, only ever sunshine shining through my life, and even when darkness fell their seemed to always be a bright light shining high. Paula was such a loving and caring soul and would do anything for anyone but was always plagued by jealous people and so many haters that didn't know her. If they did, they would never have done and said what they said to her.

Unfortunately, after her sudden and devastating passing, which absolutely killed me, my world had suddenly fell apart and my life ended with Paula gone. But these haters suddenly turned their hate to me and what made it worse was some of Paula's close friends who were anti bullying and condemned them all for the abuse and life they had seen their friend had to endure these bullies had put Paula through, but suddenly joined forces with them and helped fuel the hatred against me. I was getting slated by everyone and so many malicious rumours were being passed around about me and malicious vile name calling, but this could have all been prevented if some of Paula's friends had spoken up and let others know that I did exist and was real, but their silence and denying my existence just fuelled the hatred even more to the extent I had attempts on my life and threats to my life; I couldn't even go to the shops as I was getting spat on and verbally abused.

The threats and vile messages carried on and the still silence from people that knew about me and Paula which subsequently led to others joining the hate campaign and more lies were being printed in papers about me and over social media, which led to people on witch hunts for me and looking for me to physically hurt me but still silence from people that knew about me and Paula. From this moment on, I knew people were going to deny my existence and not tell others I was real and was with Paula and how happy we both were and how much in love we were and because of this denial and stories which were all lies coming out now it ultimately led to me not be able to say my final farewell to the woman I am so in love with, due to knowing people were there just to hurt me and look like heroes in front of others because they didn't know the truth because of the denial and silence about me.

I had no one to turn to because people were believing stories and lies. All this affected me really badly, then out the blue one person give me a lifeline and didn't believe everything that was being said and realised from Paula's conversations that I did exist and was real, and this person was Lee Wortley, the man writing this book for Paula. Alone, this man set out to clear my name, but struggled as people wouldn't speak to him about it because there was too many against me. But with sheer determination to declare my innocence this man battled on and eventually won.

I now know how Paula felt and why she had enough. I didn't know what I had done to deserve this. Why was this happening to me? When all I was guilty of was being in love and making their friend so happy and looking after her. If it wasn't for Lee I could of quite easily ended my life. I couldn't go out, I didn't know what was waiting for me and what was going to happen to me if anyone saw me. I couldn't cope anymore. I didn't know which way to turn but knew I couldn't leave Lee to try sort this out as he had stepped up for me. I couldn't sleep wondering if anyone had found out where I lived and all I kept thinking was what have I done that's so wrong that everyone hated me? I was breaking down more and more I couldn't stop crying and knew I was getting tired and didn't know how much more I could take before my body gives up but I didn't care. I was praying to Paula every night to come and take me, I really couldn't cope with all this and even more so without Paula. But at the eleventh hour (eleven months after Paula passed away) Lee opened a group and added a few people to it and within an hour the truth started to unfold and a few people that didn't know I existed were seeing this and, in all fairness, made a public apology. I actually broke down in tears because I never thought people would get the truth; I mean it took 11 months to get here and in all honesty, if it hadn't of come out when it did I really think my heart would of given up, as my heart was already broken beyond repair, because I lost Paula and to try and deal with all this hatred and vileness against me was too much. I just kept thinking I'm better off not here.

I can forgive those that didn't speak up in the beginning but not forget because of their silence and denial. It led to so much hatred towards me but these were people that are supposedly anti bullying and anti-violence but yet they done nothing to stop it and I couldn't say my final farewell to my precious Princess Paula.

Paula's Joy By Hazel Williamson (Mum)

Our Paula you were Heaven sent.
A precious jewel not given, not lent.
To us for a while that was all to brief,
Our day became night and our "Joy" became grief.
The grief will remain forever and ever,
Loving you always, forgetting you never.
But trust that when our lives are through,
We will share eternity with you.

Operation Sayers

Operation Sayers takes a detailed look at the notorious Sayers brothers rise to the top of the criminal ladder on the backstreets of Newcastle's West End and the authorities attempts to bring them crashing back to earth by any means necessary.

The Sayers family were once described by 'Northumbria Police as a 'new breed of criminal.' Brought up in the West End of Newcastle by a career criminal father and a mother who was a paid up member of Mensa they were always going to rise to the top of the criminal tree.

The book exposes corruption at the highest level, the use of drug fuelled informants, and how one member of a rival family broke the criminal code to land Stephen Sayers in court. The book also reveals for the first time the full details of 'Operation Insight' which was set up to put Stephen Sayers in jail for the rest of his life.

Available now from www.badboysbooks.net

The Sayers: Tried and Tested At The Highest Level

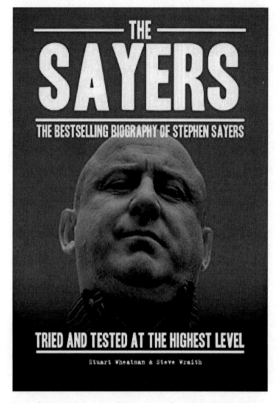

Stephen Sayers is one of the most feared men in the country, with a reputation that's preceded him in the dozens of prisons he's served time.

The Sayers family have been known on the streets of Tyneside for decades. No one else comes close to their level and it is widely known that they 'run Newcastle'. Rumoured to be behind countless violent multi-million pound armed robberies, unsolved gangland murders, extortion rackets and organised crime in general, Stephen, his brothers and associates are an unstoppable force. They've remained tight-lipped about their exploits… until now.

Stephen earned respect at an early age, blazing his own trail and coming out on top by any means necessary. A true bad lad in every sense, he gives us a first-hand account of growing up as a Sayers and living up to the reputation that the name holds.

Available now from www.badboysbooks.net

Unfinished Business

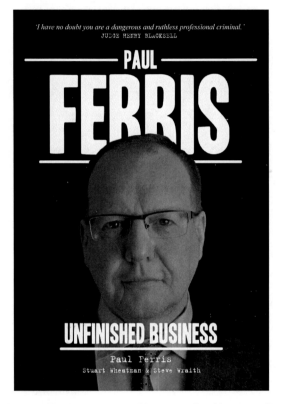

Unfinished Business was an idea conceived between Paul Ferris and writing partner Reg McKay. But Reg passed away in 2009, and the project was unfinished.

Three years later, a new alliance was formed between Ferris and true crime writers, Stuart Wheatman and Steve Wraith and the idea was reimagined. Paul wanted to pay tribute to Reg while revisiting the notion that he still had things he wanted to say. The book evolved.

In his most revealing book to date, Ferris finishes the journey he and Reg embarked upon. With his life of crime now behind him, he revisits key moments in his criminal career and replays them through philosophical eyes. He calls time on the gangster image, dispelling the myths surrounding organised crime in his city, and lifts the lid on his affiliation with Arthur Thompson – the so-called Godfather of Glasgow.

Available now from www.badboysbooks.net

Irish Criminal: The True Story Of Brendan Quinn

This is the incredible story of a man the Dutch government described as the most ruthless Irish criminal ever to walk dutch soil.
The book takes the reader through hostage situations, armed robberies and the most daring and successful prison breaks from the countries top maximum security prisons.
Meet Brendan Quinn....The Irish Criminal

Available now from www.badboysbooks.net

Paul Massey: A Salford Heart

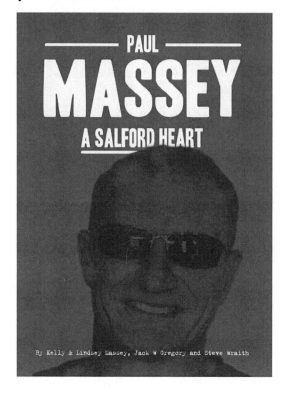

Paul Massey was gunned down on his doorstep on the 26th July 2015. He left behind a devastated family to pick up the pieces of their shattered lives. This book is a frank and honest account of Paul's life and paints a colourful picture of the loveable family man from Salford.

There is an in depth look at some of Paul's trials and tribulations and tributes from family, friends and celebrity associates such as Peter Hook, Bez and Bruce Jones.

Paul was labelled as the Mr Big of Manchester. This book dispels that myth and shows that he was a loving father and grandfather with a Salford heart.

Available now from www.badboysbooks.net